30 Before 30

ANGIE BANICKI

CONTENTS

BARCELONA

ITALY

AMSTERDAM

FOR MUSICAL INSPIRATION

Head to my Spotify 30Before30 Folder at
http://open.spotify.com/user/30before30
to add to your reading experience!

FOR MY MOM & DAD

...who always nurtured the nerd in me that made it
possible to write this book. I am so grateful that
we were able to become travelers together.

INTRODUCTION
UNDER THE INFLUENCE OF PAULO COELHO

• •

"I DREAM MY PAINTING AND THEN PAINT MY DREAM"

- Vincent Van Gogh

FROM **Angie Banicki**
TO **Angie Banicki**
subject **30 Before 30**

Dear Friend,

As I near my 30th birthday, I find myself very happy with my career, my life choices, and the friendships and work relationships I've made. I am writing to you because at some point in my life you contributed to this happiness in at least one of the above. I feel very lucky to have such amazing people around me who have touched my life. With that said, I've found there's something I still seem to be searching for to truly feel complete before blowing out the candles on my 30th. I'm writing to ask you to help me create my first trip to Europe by providing me with a glance at one of your fondest memories.

I will be traveling in July to spend 30 days with 30 experiences and I would be honored to include your moment into my trip. I want to go to places where others have found inspiration whether on their first trip, most memorable trip, or at their favorite spot to visit. I plan to document my "30 Before 30" trip and hope, as someone who has made an impact on my life, you'll be a part of my adventure! Below are a few questions to help you describe your experience. I urge you to be as simple or as creative as you'd like. Thanks in advance and you'll be hearing from me before or along the way! My plan is to hit the following five cities:

LONDON, AMSTERDAM, PARIS, BARCELONA, ROME

• What was your first memory of one of the above cities? Where'd you go and why?

• Where did you meet someone new and unexpectedly?

• If you were traveling alone, where would you go back to revisit? A restaurant, specific street, museum, hotel, or park bench....

• Do you know someone there I should go see? When people ask me about New York City, I say go meet Frankie the owner of Rao's because he sparks challenging conversation, he makes you feel part of a family, and you leave with a full stomach and a bigger heart.

• If you've visited in July, was there a specific event or tradition you took part in?

• Are you going to be there in July? If so, could I meet you along my journey?

Thanks!

Angie

I hit SEND, and my heart leapt.

30 Before 30. Thirty days in Europe. Thirty inspired moments of adventure to live it up before my 30th birthday. Just the idea of it gave me purpose. Here was a reminder that I could choose a new path, even if it was only for 30 days.

A little background first.

Ten years ago, if you had told me that at 29, a normal week for me would be taking Sienna Miller out for a night on the town, going to see an NBA Lakers game across the court from Jack Nicholson, and taking a celebrity-filled private jet to Vegas for a Maroon 5 concert, I would have laughed and said, "Order me another shot, crazypants"– of course, secretly hoping you were right.

I was the dorkypants, growing up. I was the one who saved her way to college by working shifts at our local Pizza Hut in Oregon, Illinois.

I didn't miss a single class at Northwestern—they cost a lot of money and, come rain, shine, sloshed, or half asleep, I got my pants in that seat. Hardworking and literally corn-fed, I guess you might say I was earnest and driven from the get-go.

After college, I headed to LA, not knowing what my dream job would be. Do any of us ever, really? I just wanted to be around people who had achieved their own success and would let me learn from them. I landed a job at the Elizabeth Glaser Pediatric AIDS Foundation. Inspiration number one was my first boss at EGPAF, Joel Goldman. I'd met Joel in college and was fascinated by the way he connected people. He'd meet someone and find a way to bring that person into his life. Soon, I was doing the same: "Joel, I met Ashton Kutcher last night at Skybar and he wants to come to our next fundraiser!" I liked connecting the cause with the people—and in doing that whenever I could, I found myself becoming a natural networker.

I went on to run the talent relations department at the luxury PR firm Harrison & Shriftman. Working in the world of celebrity and PR, I was amazed to see how much value was assigned to these relationships. I never understood the tabloid nature of it all. I just liked the people and the challenge of getting to meet them. I liked being around hardworking, successful actors with interesting stories—stories I was privileged to hear, not in watered-down form in US Weekly, but with all the sentiment and humanity from the storytellers themselves.

Suddenly I was throwing huge events like Michael Jordan's 40th birthday party in Vegas, and giving celebrities like Bruce Willis the newest BlackBerry. The small town girl was now getting a lot of attention. I basked in the "RSVP to Angie Banicki," and allowed myself to become that PR "it" girl.

But with that long sought-after advancement came unexpected

problems. Life started to be all about the who, and I was losing myself to that who—and for what?

I started resenting my bosses, and then myself. It wasn't that I didn't love the work—I thrived on connecting people. But somewhere amidst all the parties and the bubbly and the stuff, I had lost my own connection, to myself and to others.

I knew things were bad when I had a huge professional win, packing the *Playboy* Superbowl party with every celebrity on their wish list—Bradley Cooper, Alyssa Milano, Kevin Connelly, and girls from The Hills…and on and on. Instead of being elated, I was exhausted. The 24/7 schedule and the constant demands of clients and bosses had caught up with me, and I found myself wondering more and more: "Is this really my dream life?"

THE POWER OF SATURN'S RETURN

ACCORDING TO ASTROLOGERS, A FEELING OF RESTLESSNESS WHILE TRANSITIONING FROM YOUR 20S TO 30S IS PRETTY NORMAL. THIS PERIOD, THE SATURN RETURN, IS THE FIRST TIME THE PLANET SATURN COMPLETES ITS CYCLE THROUGH YOUR BIRTH CHART AND RETURNS TO THE SPOT IT OCCUPIED WHEN YOU WERE BORN. IT'S TRADITIONALLY A TIME OF ENDINGS AND NEW BEGINNINGS. DURING THIS TIME, MOST PEOPLE TURN INWARD AND REFLECT ON THEIR NEEDS AND DESIRES, AND THE ROLE THEY WANT TO PLAY ON THE WORLD'S STAGE.

You might chalk it up to a career that was overly concerned with the superficial. That was there, sure, but I wasn't alone in my feeling that something was missing in my life. Other friends my age, in all kinds of different careers, were going through the same thing. My coworker told me that this was an astrological phenomenon that happens to a lot of people at 30: the Saturn return.

I'd never really been into astrology, but finding a name for my

14

disorder and hearing that others experienced it too gave me relief. I was constantly asking myself: "What do I do now? What's next? What do I want life to give me?"

Mom Banicki says this passion project, the 30 Before 30, was creating itself over time. Maybe, but it hit my conscious mind like lightning. I woke up that morning and said, "I dreamt it. I'm going to Europe and I'm going to collect inspiration for my trip." I sensed that travel was my answer, but there was another important piece to it: I'd ask the people I admired and who knew me best to build my itinerary for my European voyage—to provide an inspired moment from their own travel experience that would help to create mine. I had seen the letter in my dream.

I sent that letter out, prepared for rejection—or worse, no response at all. Best to keep expectations low; this wasn't a coveted party invite.

But boy, did I get something back. Overwhelmed and over the moon is how I felt as I read the email responses. Paulo Coelho said it best: "When you discover your personal legend, the world conspires to help you achieve it."

Anyone who entered my bedroom in West Hollywood saw all that inspiration spread across my white carpet. In the form of letters, emails, books, pictures, and magazine articles—I had highlighted it all—color-coded by location. Amsterdam: green, Italy: navy, Paris: pink, London: blue, Barcelona: red.

This scrapbook carpet was overwhelming (and slightly terrifying for my roommates). It made me excited, anxious, and ready to pull my hair out, all at the same time.

With every buzz of my BlackBerry, I'd jump to check it. If the subject read "30 Before 30," my heart would flip with a surge of excitement.

I got into the habit of reading these emails aloud to anyone who might listen, always wanting to share the moment with others: "Guys, mom got Dick Van Dyke to send me an email about filming 'Chitty Chitty Bang' in Germany! Listen…"

Like every adventure, there would be challenges, and I was prepared for an obstacle course. My employers threatened to take away my job, but the stress only made it clearer to me that I needed to get away. Others questioned it, but their doubts made me question how well they knew me. Some were indifferent, but that triggered my enthusiasm to convince them of my plan, even as I was in the act of defining it for myself. I fought to get those 30 days off, worked harder, and over-prepared plans to make up for leaving.

A few weeks before I left for Europe, I sat at a dinner with a mishmash of strangers in New York. My friend Elle broke the ice as we sat down: "Angie, why don't you tell everyone what you are doing next month? Go on!"

Now, I'm a talker. In fact, I talk so much they pay me to do it. But when I am in a new group of people and have to talk about me, my dorkypants self comes out and I just want to hide under the table. With the spotlight directly on me, I began stuttering details.

"Well…I am planning this trip…my first…and I emailed some friends, and…."

"Angie's going to Europe for 30 days!" Elle blurted, saving me from my awkwardness.

"That's exciting! Where are you going in Europe?" Dave, a producer from ABC, asked, perking up across the table from me.

"Well, a bit of everywhere—Barcelona, Paris, Rome…." I spoke with more confidence this time.

"She's asking all of her friends and celebrities for advice on where to go!" Elle was more excited than I was.

I laughed, taking the spotlight back. "I'm having inspiring people help create my trip! I got an email from Jason Reitman today about his first trip to London."

Before I knew it, everyone was chiming in. In the middle of explaining my Barcelona emails, Dave jumped up, "You have to go to the top of the Sagrada Familia! I have the funniest story of climbing it!" This spawned two more Sagrada stories, and soon everyone was laughing and sharing and arguing over the best stories and, "no you havvvve to go here!" moments.

I realized my connections helped plan the trip, but these moments, grounded by the memories of Travel Past and charged with the prospect of Travel Future, connected people. That night at dinner as I watched these strangers getting to know each other over their shared experiences of foreign lands, I had no doubt that I was on the starting line to a whole new adventure.

This book contains some of the most memorable of my moments in Europe, along with the people who inspired them. I hope they will inspire you to craft your own whirlwind 30 Before 30—or 40 before 40, 50, 60....

Let the journey be never-ending.

TRIPPING POINT

Travel creates connection. Let the people who inspire you help map out your trip. The ones who matter will answer your call to adventure.

London

CHAPTER 2 TEATIME AND THE MAGNA CARTA

DESTINATION St Martins Lane, London
INSPIRATION Hollywood power couple, producer Holly
Wiersma and Cassian Elwes—agent and brother to "Princess
Bride"'s Cary Elwes—kidnap me at the airport.

● ● ● ● ● ● ● ● ● ● ● ● ● ● ● ● ● ● ●

Travel journals in hand. BlackBerry out and emails loading.
Adrenaline pumping through me as John Lennon sang through my
earphones. I'd arrived!

I bounced off the plane and it was though the sound of music
stopped short. Floods of people and unpleasant smells bombarded
me. Adventure Angie disappeared. The reality of traveling alone hit me
as I lugged my Patron duffle through Heathrow. (Yes—I was traveling
with a Patron-labeled bag, given to me by a friend of a friend who
worked with the tequila brand.)

*Where am I? Mom? What was I thinking when I thought traveling
alone was a good idea?*

Wide-eyed, confused and torn, I wanted to sit down on the ground
and cry. Missing a night of sleep will do that. Going back and forth
between feeling like a child, versus solo career woman sent into
bohemia, I followed signs for the train shuttle, doing everything in my
power not to phone an assistant, demand a car-service pickup, and
insist the hotel be notified of my arrival. That's how I worked things out
in my old world—but in this one I was giving self-reliance a try. My brain
wanted to start plotting next moves, but it was instead hitting a lot of
question marks.

On family vacations, this was the stage where everyone wonders
aloud: "How far to our hotel? What are we going to do first? What are

FROM Holly Wiersma
TO   Angie Banicki
subject **Arrival**

> Don't get on the Heathrow Express. You are being picked up by
> a driver and brought to the Elwes estate. Meet him at Gate 3.

all the numbers and questions on these passport forms?"

"Mom, stop stressing, we're on vacation. Dad, just pay the guy and stop counting how much you're spending in your head!"

"JJ, can you please stop making jokes and help me with this luggage?"

"Adam, don't be so grumpy. Jeez. Fine. We'll go eat at the restaurant you want."

"Will you all please just hurry up—this is not that complicated!"

OK, I didn't miss that part—the traveling and balancing personalities!

I started to relax. Traveling alone just might be amazing.

I looked down and saw my cell battery dying.

I am an adventurer.

Nope. Still scared shitless. I wanted to go back to the white carpet of my apartment, surrounded by the color-coded journals, planning my travel. The "build up and pretend" stage was so much more fun. My eyes, trained for spotting outlets, start scanning the walls to charge my BlackBerry while my brain plotted how I'd handle getting a train. I wasn't about to ask for help.

Before I had time to panic, my BlackBerry flashed! It was a text from my friend from home, the great Holly Wiersma, producer and wife of the agent Cassian Elwes:

"Don't get on the Heathrow Express. You are being picked up by a driver and brought to the Elwes estate. Meet him at Gate 3."

BIO ▶▶

HOLLY WIERSMA & CASSIAN ELWES

Holly Wiersma and Cassian Elwes have always been a reality show to me. They live in the Hollywood Hills with their seven dogs—untrained. Producing the show is Prince Moses, the alpha pup who has a full wardrobe of dog outfits and his own cartoon strip. Four foot, eleven inch Holly is a social engine. Always in 6-inch heels that balance her 100-pound frame, she runs around her house throwing parties and barbeques for her celebrity friends while still negotiating film deals at the same time.

But Cassian and Holly are a lot more interested in great movies than in reality TV. Cassian has produced 53 movies and shows, including "Blue Valentine" and Margin Call." Holly has eight producing credits herself, including the critically acclaimed "Bobby," written and directed by Emilio Estevez.

If they really were a reality show, my episode with them would be called "HOLLY AND CASSIAN: THE LONDON SPECIAL...Guest starring Angie Banicki."

I let out a huge sigh. I felt like a child who'd found mom after being lost in the supermarket maze. I felt my shoulders drop and the bag slide from my arm. Self-reliance is great, but I knew I had plenty of time for that on the trip.

This first surprise was quickly followed by a second. The "driver" at Gate 3 was Cassian himself, in a tiny European car, with Holly in the passenger seat.

"Angie Banicki! Welcome! We are going to take you to the place where the Magna Carta was signed—in Cassian's backyard." Voila, a surprise moment to start the trip!

We pulled up to the grounds and drove through a grandiose wooden gate then down a dirt path.

Holly and Cassian tour-guided me down the road, just as they tend to tour-guide me through the film world in Hollywood.

Cassian's family welcomed me, despite being in the throes of preparations for Cassian's sister's wedding. In a constant state of awe, and more than a little jet lagged, I felt innocent and vulnerable in these new surroundings. Tents were going up and Cassian's sister and mom were voicing concerns about the placement of the kids' table, hanging the dress under the high ceilings to let the wrinkles fall, and positioning flowers at the entry.

I sheepishly looked back out the door, a view stretching into the warm UK sun.

"Angie Banicki, you are so quiet! Aren't you excited to be here? Do you see, over there is the field where the Magna Carta was signed!" Holly pointed and said in her sing-songy voice, seeming to sense I wasn't myself.

"Angie, it's unbelievable. You've arrived on one of London's very few perfect, sunny days. This is very uncommon," says Cassian, his accent seeming stronger as I listened to him in his home country.

Cassian accompanied us, joking about all the knickknacks his mother had squirreled away over the years and, "insists on spreading around the home."

"Mother, she doesn't need to see all the rooms!"

Funny to see Cassian, now the embarrassed son, worrying that his mother was taking up too much of a friend's time with "Mom stuff." Meanwhile I treasured the history and, despite the magnitude of the place, felt a gentle sense of home as Mum walked me through it.

Though she is older and moves more slowly than her grown children, Mum thrived on my fascination and eagerly walked about the house, describing the invaluable artifacts in each new room we encountered. Sharing them with me seemed to breathe new life into them, and her. All moms want to be appreciated, especially by their own kids. When they can't get their kids to feel it, a friend of their child is the second best thing. And of course, Mum knows best: The tour was exactly what I needed as I tried to acclimate.

Jet lag was setting in, and just as I was getting loopy with tiredness, Cassian and Holly volunteered to drive me to my hotel, St Martins Lane. On the way to the city, they took me for fish and chips at their favorite spot. Over beers, Cass unraveled more of his family story for me.

His parents met in the UK when Tessa was 17, and his dad, an English portrait painter, was 23.

His grandfather (Tessa's father) had a court restraining order placed against his dad, making it impossible for them to marry. The couple ended up fleeing to Cuba to elope, but soon after the ceremony had to board a raft to Miami to escape the revolution. The hotel where they were staying as guests of the mobster Meyer Lansky was raided 20 minutes after they left. To make sure their marriage was legal, they had a second ceremony in front of New York's Supreme Court. Tessa is the niece of diplomat and Yugoslav shipping magnate Vane Ivanovic and

THE MAGNA CARTA

THE MAGNA CARTA WAS SIGNED IN A MEADOW IN SOUTHERN ENGLAND IN 1215, YET LAID THE FOUNDATION FOR CITIZENS' RIGHTS AS WE KNOW THEM TODAY. THE DOCUMENT, WHICH LISTED 37 LAWS, LIMITED THE POWER OF KING JOHN AND FUTURE ROYALS, ALLOWING FOR THE FORMATION OF A POWERFUL PARLIAMENT AND ESTABLISHING DUE PROCESS AND THE RIGHT TO HABEAS CORPUS. LESS KNOWN WAS THAT THE MAGNA CARTA PUT AN END TO THE ROYAL SEX TRADE; PRIOR TO ITS SIGNING, THE KING COULD SELL THE WIDOWS AND DAUGHTERS OF BARONS AS WIVES WHEN IN NEED OF EXTRA FUNDING.

great-great-niece of Dušan Popovi, one of the founders of Yugoslavia. The elopement was a major cause célèbre at the time, arousing widespread controversy.

I had never heard Cass open up so freely and honestly about his family and I was touched to be let in on the story. I felt my head relax in all the history and romance. What a fairytale surprise to kickoff London!

TRIPPING POINT

Castles or cornfields, we are most ourselves in our
homes—take every chance you can to
meet people there.

CHAPTER 3 PIECES OF SILVER

DESTINATION The Tate Modern, London
INSPIRATION Minnie Driver sends me to teatime, Michelle Trachtenberg likes antiques, but it's the need for air-conditioning that leads me to the day's real treasure.

● ● ● ● ● ● ● ● ● ● ● ● ● ● ● ● ● ● ●

My body launched out of bed, breaking free from the tightly wrapped white sheets of the soft comfortable hotel bed at the St Martins Lane in Soho. Waking up in a new city with a day full of possibilities gave me a bolt of energy, and surprisingly I felt no jet lag. Thank God for this because I had quite the lineup of moments planned. I jumped out of bed, almost embarrassed by the peppy self that hadn't emerged from the sheets in quite some time. This London day was mine for the taking.

I started the day with what became my "normal" planning process: flipping through my color-coded journal, cross-referencing it with the new suggestions that kept showing up daily in my BlackBerry, bouncing those off maps and whatever meet-ups I had already planned and scheduled on my calendar, and trying to arrive at something more-or-less manageable. Today's agenda was shaping up like this: tea at the Orangery, Portobello Road for antiquing, Wimbledon in the afternoon (tickets still unconfirmed!), and finally, the Tate Modern.

First stop, the Tube to Kensington for Minnie Driver's recommended tea spot, Queen Anne's 18th-century Orangery. Walking up to the garden, the pathway was surrounded by greenery. I noticed plenty of regulars on their morning walks—some with strollers, others with dogs.

Sitting and having tea, alone in the beautiful gardens, I felt like a true world traveler enjoying a haven of heavenly peace. I methodically poured tea while observing the family at the table next to me. Two young boys in sear-sucker suits sat nearby, eating chocolate croissants while their parents spoke in heavy British accents. I felt myself sitting up straighter. Yes, I could be proper. I smoothed out the bed head that my hotel's gay concierge, who I consulted for London-ready fashion advice, had kindly called, "just tousled enough." Then the mum scolded her boys for bouncing around the table, completing this caricature of British reserve.

After an hour of tea sipping and quiet observation, I set off for Portobello Road on what, according to my maps, seemed to be a walk able route. I felt sweat start to drip down my side and my scalp, adding

FROM **Michelle Trachtenberg**
TO   **Angie Banicki**
subject **30 Before 30**

Angie,

One of my favorite cities in the world to visit is London, England. I love the people, the architecture, the shopping, and the history. There is so much to see in London, it's hard to pick just one spot. Of course I highly recommend going to Buckingham palace and trying to make the guards laugh, close to impossible, but worth a try!! My favorite little secret in London though, is the antique market called Portobello Road in Knotting Hill. Every Saturday Portobello Rd. becomes an outside flea market. A loooooong line of antique and vintage dealers line the street selling some of the most unique accessories and clothes you'll ever find. You feel like you're digging through a treasure chest or history book. I can guarantee anything you find there will be extra special and carry its very own story! I think that's the best souvenir from London. Enjoy!

X

BIO ▶▶

a new layer to my fashionable "tousle." I pulled the rubber band off my wrist and went for the pony, worth it for the cool breeze on my neck. My posture, perfected at tea, was now bending in my push toward my next destination.

To add to the disenchantment of it all, mid-walk I got an email: the Wimbledon ticket I had hoped to have for later that day was a no-go. Bloody hell!

After more twists and turns and checks to the BlackBerry maps, I finally found Portobello. It started with the library, which I snapped for Mom Banicki, the librarian. I knew she would appreciate that I found her favorite place on day two.

As I ventured forward into the main section of Portobello, crammed with people, the sweat was back and now felt like it was mixing with sweat spritzing off the others around me. I couldn't wait for all this to mix with the grime of antiques. (Truthfully, antiques had never been my thing, but I was trying new things, right?)

Michelle Trachtenberg described the long road lined with antique

FROM Minnie Driver
TO   Angie Banicki
subject **30 Before 30**

Go for tea in the Orangery in Kensington gardens, then walk through the park to Notting Hill and down the Portobello road and market (market is on Friday and sat). Any pub that has a garden is worth stopping for a pint of Guinness....a pint in London is a must as it is totally different from beer in America...

In Paris I fell in love at sunset outside Notre Dame....I then proceeded to walk around the Marais all night. If you are looking at Notre Dame, walk to the left and follow the street along the side of the cathedral till you get to a bridge., cross over and you will now be headed into the Jewish quarter or 'Marais' it is stunning and filled with falafel, shops and beautiful streets.

PORTOBELLO ROAD, LONDON

THE WORLD'S LARGEST ANTIQUES MARKET, ON A STREET IN THE NOTTING HILL DISTRICT OF THE ROYAL BOROUGH OF KENSINGTON AND CHELSEA. THE MARKET IS OPEN EVERY SATURDAY, AND SHOPS ARE OPEN SIX DAYS A WEEK. PORTOBELLO WAS KNOWN BEFORE 1740 AS GREEN'S LANE, A COUNTRY ROAD THROUGH OPEN FIELDS AND ORCHARDS. IN THE VICTORIAN ERA, THE ROAD AND URBAN LANDSCAPE OF SHOPS AND MARKETS BEGAN TO DEVELOP. IN THE WINTER OF 1927, GEORGE ORWELL TOOK RESIDENCE THERE. THE ROAD IS HOME TO ONE OF BRITAIN'S OLDEST CINEMAS AND HOSTS ITS OWN ANNUAL FILM FESTIVAL. IT HAS BEEN THE SETTING FOR A CAT STEVENS SONG AND A PAULO COELHO NOVEL.

ORANGERY

QUEEN ANNE'S 18TH-CENTURY ORANGERY, IN THE HEART OF KENSINGTON GARDENS—ONCE THE SETTING FOR THE MOST LAVISH OF COURT ENTERTAINMENTS—IS THE PERFECT LOCATION FOR AN ELEGANT LUNCH OR AN INDULGENT AFTERNOON TEA, WITH OVER TEN DIFFERENT VARIETIES TO CHOOSE FROM. IT HAS VIEWS OF THE PALACE AND SITS AMIDST ELEGANT GARDENS. IT HAS BEEN TRADITIONAL SINCE MEDIEVAL TIMES FOR THE MONARCH TO DISTRIBUTE GIFTS OF SPECIALLY MINTED COINS TO POOR PEOPLE ON MAUNDY THURSDAY. THIS NOW TAKES PLACE IN CHURCHES AROUND THE COUNTRY, BUT QUEEN ANNE HELD THE MAUNDY CEREMONY IN THE ORANGERY.

THE ORANGERY WAS OFTEN USED FOR CEREMONIES. QUEEN ANNE WAS NOTABLE AS THE LAST MONARCH WHO PERFORMED THE CEREMONY CALLED "TOUCHING THE KING'S EVIL" WHERE PEOPLE WITH DISEASES BELIEVED THAT BY BEING PHYSICALLY TOUCHED BY THE MONARCH THEY WOULD BE CURED.

vendors as, "digging through a treasure chest or history book." Maybe it was my mood, but all this stuff on display, being picked over, just made me think about the celebrity gifting suites I'd worked back at home. At star-studded events like Sundance and the Grammies, many companies will pay for a booth with freebies of their products—BlackBerries, jewelry, makeup, you name it—to give to the celebrities who attend the suite. Basically, it's free stuff for rich people, and when you work a suite, you have to be a "NO" person—telling people, "No, sorry, you don't get a free BlackBerry." I am not a good "NO" person.

I tried to shut down all these negative thoughts and enjoy the genius adventure itinerary I had carefully planned. But I couldn't fake excitement in these treasures. It was time to take Minnie's second, safer piece of advice: "A pint in London is different than in America." I'd cleanse myself of this whole experience by grabbing a beer. (Same way I handled those gifting suites, actually—escape to the bar.) When I got to the bar, though, the tennis match was on. Another sweaty slap in the face. I chugged one down.

Now it was time to get into a cab and tackle the Tate—on the other side of town. Right now, its primary appeal wasn't culture. It was air conditioning. I headed through the doors feeling like I was at least doing my duty as a tourist, but I still couldn't shut down self-critical Angie in my head, analyzing: "Why aren't I enjoying this more? Was this the right way to find what I wanted to find, or would a nice Lonely Planet book have been better? Am I truly the adventurer I thought?"

After some time exploring on my own, I happened upon a small group walking with a tour guide. I secretly listened in and found myself relaxing. I was just happy to have someone with some authority telling me what was interesting and why for the first time that day. I decided to become part of their tour.

I was with them for maybe a minute when the guide announced the next stop: "30 Pieces of Silver." I stopped walking, not believing I'd heard him right. But then I saw the sign as we walked into the room with the exhibit. Mesmerized by the concept and the beautiful design, I veered off to be alone. It actually wasn't a choice. The silver was a magnet, pulling me with a force as strong as my earlier uncertainty. Not only because of the name of the exhibit, but because it was different than anything I'd ever seen.

Cornelia Parker, a British artist, had taken 30 pieces of silver and transformed them from trash into art—here, finally, was the treasure I had been sent to Portobello Road to find. She collected silver, from junkyards to antique stores, and then had it flattened by steamrollers. Sentimental items such as trophies and wedding gifts once valued for their memories were crushed to indistinguishable pieces. Dinnerware to trombones, reduced to the same flat pieces of metal, dangling from the ceiling with strings, in 30 formations, each with light above to enhance their luster. High, low, beautiful, practical—now it all was part of this mesmerizing, shimmering vision working its magic on me. The final effect of the artist's surreal poetry spoke to the "ephemeral and fluid appearance" of the silver. The flattening all of these pieces were acts of violence—and yet were necessary to expose and deconstruct the layers of meaning within the remains.

What would my 30 pieces of silver be? I thought about my sweaty rejection of Portobello Road that day. I needed to be broken down to discover my own layers. I had gotten so used to grinning and bearing it in the gifting suites and all their equivalents. It was time to throw myself at new things and not judge myself when I didn't like them. I needed those disappointments to learn how to recognize what it felt like when something really did click.

TRIPPING POINT

Reset your expectations. Not every moment of travel is perfect bliss. Without judgment, try a little bit of everything. It's all part of the experience.

CHAPTER 4 TRAINING DAY

DESTINATION Bar Italia, London
INSPIRATION Harley Pasternak, fitness trainer to the stars, sends me to his favorite breakfast spot.

• • • • • • • • • • • • • • • • • • •

When Harley Pasternak, fitness trainer to the stars, gives advice, you take it. If Halle Berry's body is listening then you bet your bottom, mine will too.

The first two mornings in London, I rolled out from beneath my crisp white sheets and quickly dressed to go hunt my usual hot espresso and buttery croissant. That rolled up ball of butter and batter became my splash of water to the face the entire trip. The fattening pastry was exactly what my body needed and craved for all the miles I clocked walking, running, and exploring on my trip. Needless to say, I was thankful to forgo the cookie and cheap American coffee that was my everyday a.m. fuel back at home. (Harley would be appalled.) What I realize now is that establishing this new ritual of coffee and croissants gave me a familiar routine that anchored me so that I could be calm and present in the fun chaos that defines travel.

On my third London morning, London blue journal in hand, I headed to find Harley's recommended spot, the Bar Italia. I didn't get far before I was hit by a quick, hard splash of rain to my face with the perfect amount of cold to make me forget the cocktails from the night before. So this is the rain I'd heard so much about. I pulled open the glass door and heard an old-fashioned bell ring from above my head.

subject **Re: 30**

OK,

So you have to go to Bar Italia in London.

It's in Soho.

I really feel like time stands still when you are there. It is really a true example of authenticity. Something we forget about in Hollywood. Everything is real. It just is, it's not contrived. Here are some notes I took to describe it...

1950s feel

Boxing poster on wall

No skim milk

No Splenda

No low fat apple tart

Custard tart and cannolis

Old NCR cash register

Italian barista

Coin operated "bacci" gumball machine

Bar with bar stools, no tables (other than outside)

Mirror along wall of bar...allows u to see all of bar and forces u to see yourself.

Floor reminds me of floor from day school, worn tile

Old "tube" televisions playing soccer games

So sell fresh smoothies and juice

Bar at back with exclusively Italian liquors (Campari, martini,)

Paninis

Old gaggia machine with long pull levers

Sitting down with an espresso and large orange juice, the stool where I sat faced a mirrored wall—perfect for observation of the place, not so perfect for observation of myself so early in the morning. I reread Harley's email and looked for the points he mentioned—gumball machine, boxing poster—while also sneaking glances at the bartender/barista preparing for his day. His moves were slow and methodical but executed with such pure enjoyment. His white teeth sparkled under his grin as he wiped counters, checked coffee, and arranged chairs. It was like out of a '50s ad shot in an ice cream parlor. He had a bounce that no coffee could ever give me—and it was authentic, just the way Harley described the place to be.

Bar Italia on day three is where I first felt life start to slow down. Was it because Harley had described it that way, or was it truly the atmosphere of the place? Both, I think. I didn't look at my BlackBerry. Didn't notice the time. Didn't think about all the things I wanted to accomplish that day. Just reveled in the simple. Hot espresso. Fresh O.J. A man delighting in his daily routine. Seeing a new place through the eyes of a friend.

I smiled in the mirror at the man behind the bar as he caught my eye, as if to let me know it was okay to be alone observing life through that mirror. Then he went back to the kitchen, and I listened to the muted sounds of their Italian.

TRIPPING POINT

Authenticity and orange juice make good companions.
Slow down and enjoy the details.

BIO ▶▶

HARLEY PASTERNAK

Funny thing, I've never actually gotten a Harley workout—only a virtual one. We did a demo together once for Harley's "Hollywood Workout" for WiiFit. We ran side by side in place, got our BMIs together—it was fun, but maybe not as intense as the motions he puts his celeb clients like Lady Gaga, Megan Fox, and Robert Pattinson through. But while he hasn't cheered me on through physical training, he was a huge help in keeping me going through the struggles of this book, providing words of encouragement all along the way.

CHAPTER 5 NOT YOUR DANDY

DESTINATION Colony Room, London

INSPIRATION Fashionista Dayna Zegarelli sends me to meet her Dandy.

● ● ● ● ● ● ● ● ● ● ● ● ● ● ● ● ● ●

"**D**o you want to meet a dandy?" Dayna excitedly touted.

Do I want to meet a dandy?

"Yes, I'm in! Wait….what's a Dandy?"

Dayna Z is intimidating. Her sarcastic wit, obscene humor, and daunting laugh is only slightly softened by an air of fabulous fashionista. I have always wanted to be a little bit more like Dayna.

I figured a dandy was probably some sort of British mascot, pop culture comedian, or fashion guru, but in truth she never quite told me. She only laughed and said, "You will love my dandy!"

Put most simply, a dandy is a male clothes horse—but actually it's a cultural movement that goes back to the 1790s. Here was Albert Camus' later take:

"'To live and die before a mirror': that, according to Baudelaire, was the dandy's slogan. It is indeed a coherent slogan... The dandy…is always compelled to astonish. Singularity is his vocation, excess his way to perfection. Perpetually incomplete, always on the fringe of things, he compels others to create him, while denying their values. He plays at life because he is unable to live it."

Hmmm. Perhaps I should Wikipedia Dayna's dandy, Sebastian Horsley:

"Sebastian Horsley (born August 8, 1962) is a London artist best known for having undergone a voluntary crucifixion. Horsley's writings often revolve around his dysfunctional family, his drug addictions, sex, and his reliance on prostitutes."

Yikes. Oddly entertaining. Sounds like half of LA....

I like a good character and after working in Hollywood, I'd learned not to pay too much attention to what I read in the press. I prefer to make my own judgments.

Then I got this email from Dayna's dandy, Sebastian Horsley, as I tucked into bed on day four:

FROM **Sebastian Horsley**
TO **Angie Banicki**
subject **RE: Hi!!!**

Hello Darling,
Are you pretty? Me too.
Tomorrow night or Tuesday night?
Come to my room at 7.00 p.m. If you're late, I'll start without you.
Sx

I sat up in bed, heartbeat picked up.

Not sure how to respond, I went with light and fun, despite the frightening images I'd seen on the web. Mostly I was curious—and excited. I responded in a way I thought would show that I was too dorky for this dandy's delight.

"Of course I'm pretty, you big goof! Tomorrow works."

Just a big goof who nails himself to crosses, right?

What in God's name had I gotten myself into?

That next London morning started off the same as any other—sunny then rainy and with me downing a green tea and a skinny ginger muffin from the Starbucks across from my hotel. I was already starting to feel overwhelmed by London–too many people to meet and every day, more and more suggestions of where to go. The adventure was turning into a job and I was burning the midnight oil.

As I sifted through the blue highlights in my London journal, I debated where to go next. Without even thinking about it, I found myself googling Sebastian again and my heart rate popped back up. Horsley ran a monthly column in the *Erotic Review* from 1998 to 2004. In early 2006, Horsley– together with Marion McBride–began to run a weekly sex advice column in *The Observer*. Four months later, after graphic discussions of oral and anal sex had led to numerous complaints from outraged readers, the column was discontinued.

Oh my. I shoved down the muffin and decided to get started.

I headed first to the London Eye, where the slow-moving Ferris wheel would provide a view of the city and time to plan next moves.

As I waited in line to go up on the Eye, I got another email. My stomach was doing flip-flops–and not from rising 443 feet in the air in

FROM Sebastian Horsley
TO   Angie Banicki
subject RE: Hi!!!

7 Meard Street. Soho. Come at 6.30. Or when you walk through the door.
Sx

the glass capsule ascending over London.

I chose to ignore the come when I walk through the door, or pretend to anyway.

My heartbeat and stomach settled as I listened in on my capsule mates pointing out the sights. Big Ben looming across the London River, Hyde Park–where I'd been walking earlier, and the Queen's castle—anything I could see that would distract from the dandy declarations.

As we began our descent, I attempted some photos despite the rapidly accumulating raindrops. A beautiful young mother and her little boys sharing the clear egg with me had stolen my attention. I watched the boys delight in the moving wheel and glanced down at my BlackBerry. Another email from the dandy, with yet more innuendo. No turning back.

Maybe my next tour stop should be St Paul's Cathedral. Yes, church

FROM   **Sebastian Horsley**
TO   **Angie Banicki**
subject **RE: Hi!!!**

I'll take you to the famous Colony Rooms before hand. It is one of the most famous/notorious places in London. It must be in your book.

So my dear. I am signing off now. Come to my studio at 6.30/ 7.00 p.m. tomorrow. 7 Meard Street Soho. It has a sign on the door saying "This is not a brothel." Do not believe everything you read.

Lots of love
Sx

before brothel. The rain lightened as I wandered along the water on the Jubilee Walkway, half-heartedly making my way toward the church. This would please my father—not the *Father*, but my dad. On Father's Day for the last six years, all Dad asked is that we go to mass for him and say a prayer. My intention was to take a photo or two and be on my way, but before I could get my camera out, standing in front of the huge dome, a roaring wind and sudden downpour gave me no choice but to take refuge inside the chapel.

OK, God, I get it.

The cathedral with its stained glass and vaulted ceilings, perfumed with incense and candles, embodied every image of Catholicism and evoked every emotion of spirituality I'd felt growing up. Going up the 80 flights of stairs leading to the top level of the chapel, there was no time to think about all the dandy-babble because I could only concentrate on breathing. Each landing, I'd stop to breathe and look down, inhaling the scent of the church. The familiar incenses were like Dad's hands on my shoulders as we stood in the pews saying "Our Fathers" at Mass every week.

Nerves calmed, I headed back to my hotel and shot the dandy one last email, having had the bright idea that we should meet in public rather than at his not-a-brothel brothel.

FROM **Sebastian Horsley**
TO   **Angie Banicki**
subject **RE: Hi!!!**

Can we keep it to 7? I have a 6 p.m. mtg.- one not nearly as important as you but hoping you can still squeeze me in...or we can meet at colony?

My email backfired:

FROM **Sebastian Horsley**
TO   **Angie Banicki**
subject **RE: Hi!!!**

7 fine darling. The Colony is next door to my studio. My studio was
known as an annex of the Colony for many years. And it may be
you who has to squeeze me in. God gave me unlimited girth and I
exceeded it.

I read that response as I was running out of St Martins Lane Hotel,
headed to Soho House for my pre-dandy drinks meeting, and almost
fell flat on my face.

An hour later, over the river (of champagne) and through the
wooden signs to Grandmother's house (or dare I say my grand dad-
dy's brothel) I go. I stopped in front of the door and prepared myself
for the Big Bad Wolf. I found myself quivering in my ballet flats in front
of 7 Meard Street. I looked one way, then the other, and finally stabbed
the buzzer with my outstretched finger. A windowsill above was thrown
open immediately, and out popped the head of the grand dandy himself, who daintily shouted down at me.

"Oh darling, punctual. Off to a good start."

The door buzzed and I opened it and walked up the stairs before
I could reconsider. Sebastian met me at the doorway, watching for
my reaction as he opened the door to his shrine of an apartment—a
shrine I later learned he refused to allow the likes of Kate Moss to be
photographed in. He was to be the center of attention at all times here.
Looking around I began to understand a little bit of this dandy's world.
The shrine was awash in brilliant hues of velvety rich red. It wasn't
huge, and not at all a home. It was a collection, like one seen in a mu-

seum—as a tribute to a former pop star or artist. It screamed, "Look at me. Let me shock you." There was a wall of mini skulls, one I later saw as the backdrop to his book cover. The velvety red hues bounced off the furniture to the bloody photos of the dandy's crucifixion.

"Darling, you are pretty, aren't you."

Giggling nervously, I was surprised to sense immediately that he was nervous too. I knew immediately that this man wasn't any scarier than a cartoon. We were mascot to mascot. Mirror to mirror. He had the sensibility of a little boy—one you just want to hug. Well, maybe more like a teenage boy just hitting puberty—one who doesn't know exactly how to react to women, but embraces them with adoration and the desire to be adored.

"Wow, this place has character!" I said, nervous to just get something out.

"You like it, don't you? Want to see my bed?" The dandy taunted. "Although it's not much use to me."

He followed his innuendos with a light, almost high-pitched laugh and an immediate downturn of his eyes while turning his head off to the side. His boyishness negated the actual raunchy words coming out of his mouth—and he got away with saying anything and everything because of this charm. It was apparent he just craved the attention. All I wanted was to link arms with him and humor that little boy within!

But we weren't there yet; we were still in the uncomfortable space of avoiding each others' eyes. So the dandy busily finished up his email at the small desk in the corner of the room while I began exploring, sensing this is what Mr. Horsley desired of me. His fidgeting was oddly comforting in my built-up anxiousness over the meeting.

I asked lots of questions about everything I saw. This comforted me and seemed an easy way to make conversation.

"Was your mother there for the crucifixion? Why did you do it? Who are these people in costumes?"

"Ah, yes, Mum. She was there and not so happy for her son. Father wasn't, the old bastard. It was quite the scene. Lots of attention."

"Are you really banned from the U.S.? How does that even happen? Have you even tried to enter?"

"Ahhh, the banning. That's a story for you, some of it's in my book as well."

"Wait! I want to read your book!"

He walked over and handed me a letter on U.S. government letterhead.

I looked down at the letter. It was signed by Condoleezza Rice and prohibited him from stepping foot in America. Then I noticed he had a copy of his book in his other hand.

"Oooh, a signed copy!?"

He handed over the book, and I later read in the front jacket:

Angie,
I hope you enjoy. I know you'll
read this with one hand my dear.
Welcome to London.
Love,
S xxx

THE COLONY ROOM

SEBASTIAN DESCRIBED THE COLONY ROOM IN HIS BOOK:

"WHEN I MOVED TO SOHO I SPENT THE AFTERNOONS IN THE CLUBS—IN THE COLONY ROOM, THE GROUCHO, OR THE FRENCH—I PAUSED AT THEM ALL LIKE A DEVOTEE PAUSES TO PRAY AT EACH STATION OF THE CROSS. BUT THE COLONY WAS AND WILL ALWAYS BE THE BEST. IT IS SO DELIGHTFULLY LOSER FRIENDLY.

"I ADORE THE COLONY. IT'S THE ONLY BAR THAT I KNOW WHERE PEOPLE ACTUALLY TALK TO YOU. IT IS THE ONLY BAR THAT I KNOW TO WHICH YOU CAN TURN UP TO ALONE AND BE MADE TO FEEL WELCOME. IT IS FULL OF WRITERS, ARTISTS, AND POETS—THE SORT OF PEOPLE THAT IN OTHER BARS WOULD BE CALLED DRUNKS. IT REMINDS ME OF THE TARDIS. IT'S MINUTE ON THE OUTSIDE BUT HUGE ON THE INSIDE AND YOU GO THERE FOR LOVE, WHICH THEY SERVE BY THE GLASSFUL."

I watched as Sebastian nervously unbuttoned and re-buttoned the vintage vest that completed his bright blue velour suit ensemble. This action was oddly comforting to me. I saw that he was a bit like me, comfortable with crowds but at times insecure with one-on-one. It was time to go be around people—or in his case, in front of them.

As we walked down the stairs, I got a closer look at Sebastian. His bright black hair was carefully sculpted to poke this way and that. Mascara brought out his promiscuous, glowing eyes, and a pinky red blush complemented bright red nails, completing his look for the evening. Even his walk had a specific bounce and side step to it.

"My dear, I figure we have a drink at the Colony Room and then I take you to dinner at the very prestigious Ivy." I clapped like a little girl, telling him I'd heard about the Ivy. Outside, Sebastian pointed across the street and explained to me, "That's where Rachel number two lives."

"Rachel number two?"

"Yes, I only date Rachels. Rachel number two is a prostitute."

I nod and note these facts in my head. Questions for later. A hop, skip, and jump and there we were, standing in front of the green door to the Colony Room.

The Colony Room was quite an elite and secret spot of London. Most had never heard of it, but the few who knew were very impressed that I was granted access. We were buzzed in and round the dirty steps turning along walls that were covered with signatures and old pictures of famed Brits. Inside felt like the high school basement of a friend whose parents let the kids drink in the dingy dark confines. There was no one behind the bar except an older gentleman who greeted us with firm handshakes and with an obvious affinity for Sebastian. He took our orders and then went behind the bar set up in the corner to make our drinks. It was all very dark and seeping with a certain sadness. Once a place frequented by legends, it now just carried on holding tight to every old photo and memory. Sebastian and I sat in the corner where we got past formalities and he told me about his book and life in London. I was able to hold my own with his quick wit while I sensed he was on good behavior for me. And we found commonalities despite our extremely different lifestyles.

After my vodka soda and Sebastian's just soda, we dandied our way over to the Ivy. And when I say dandied, I mean arms linked, skipping until interrupted by a slight drizzle just blocks before our destination. Sebastian, fearing he would lose his dandy flare from the raindrops, skedaddled to hide under the awnings as I doubled over laughing.

Walking through the doors of the Ivy, Sebastian was greeted like a king. We took our seats at the center table along the wall—one he explains is the only table that can see every other table in the place and, more importantly, can be seen by every table.

We talk about the Rachels. Sebastian softens when he mentions his most recent love. In his bright eyes I see he isn't used to discussing it, other than in jest.

"Rachel never wanted to sleep over but thankfully her business was only down the block."

I asked about his relationship with his parents and spoke of mine. It had been tumultuous, he said, especially with his father. He told me about attempted suicide in his family. He was well-equipped with light, ready-made stories, but when I probed him, I could see suffering in his sad eyes. I found myself telling him about my dad's brother's suicide. Most of my friends don't even know about my Uncle Joey. I was probably 11, but it was the first time I saw real raw emotion in my father, and that was when he really turned to the church.

Our bill was paid on a tab.

"How come you didn't have to pay?" By this point I felt comfortable pushing Sebastian for answers.

For the first time, Sebastian was timid in his reply as he explained he'd donated all his family's art for the second floor, and in exchange, he had a tab that would probably last him for life.

A true gentleman, Sebastian walked me back to my hotel, made sure I got in OK, pecked me on the cheek, and headed on his way.

Later, I got this email in response to my thank you:

FROM **Sebastian Horsley**
TO **Angie Banicki**
subject **RE: Hi!!!**

My darling,

A pleasure beyond measure. Wasn't it fun? I knew we would get on because of Dayna. Also I love Americans. You are so different to us aren't you? You are so literal!

Delighted that night No 4 was the ultimate and I expect it still to be by the time you finish. Do I look like a footnote? Or even a chapter? No, I look like a book. The Colony and then The Ivy. Not bad for a first trip to London. So hope you can help me get into the States. 54? Add a few noughts baby. Shall I run for president with you as first lady?

Darling, I've got to go as the Pilot team are arriving any minute but we can do a picture later or next time?

Love my dear
Sx

BIO ▶▶

SEBASTIAN HORSLEY

Sebastian Horsley passed away in 2010. He relapsed after a period of sobriety and over-dosed. From *The Guardian*'s obituary, published June 20, 2010: "Sebastian Horsley, who has been found dead aged 47, always favoured the provocative in his writing and art. In 2000, he notoriously underwent a crucifixion in the Philippines as a participant in a rebirth ceremony. He was nailed to a cross for 20 minutes, fainted from the pain and fell when the footrest gave way. The incident—photographed by Dennis Morris and filmed by the artist Sarah Lucas, with accompanying music by Gavin Rossdale, the lead singer of Bush—inspired a series of paint-ings by Sebastian. These, along with the photographs and the film, were exhibited in his 2002 show 'Crucifixion.'

"Having swum with sharks when he was young, Sebastian became fascinated by their capacity for beauty and danger, and they became a recurrent motif in his large-scale paintings. His 2007 retrospective at the Spectrum Gallery, in London, was entitled 'Hookers, Dealers, Tailors' and included displays of his flamboy-ant bespoke tailoring. The outfit-ters Turnbull & Asser created a shirt in his honour. Sebastian was as comfortable in the glitter-ing salons of London's art world as he was in the backstreet dives of Soho, where he lived."

▌ TRIPPING POINT ▐

Don't judge a dandy by his makeup.

In loving memory of Sebastian Horsley.

CHAPTER 6
TRUTH AT THE HONOR BAR

DESTINATION Honor Bar, London

INSPIRATION Talent manager Chris Huvane sends me in search of a destination so exclusive it may not even exist.

• • • • • • • • • • • • • • • • • • •

"**H**ave you ever heard of the Honor Bar?" was one of the first things out of my mouth each time I met a new person in London. The answers I got were all over the map:

"Never heard of it. I don't think that place exists." It does exist.

"Oh yeah. It's behind the Covent Garden Hotel lobby. Super chic and hot." Nope. Not there and not really.

"Yes! It's a secret underground spot. I've never been! Tell me how it is." Not underground and not really a secret.

It became a great talking piece, this mythical, magical bar. And the more random the answers, the more curious I got. Chris Huvane, the former West Coast Editor of GQ, now a talent manager, who gave me the tip, is an instigator, often of mischief. And now he had instigated a tricky adventure for me around London.

After rereading Chris's email, I first had to decipher if there was in fact an actual Covent Garden Hotel. I couldn't trust a Londoner with any information at this point and that whole part of town was still an enigma. I'd sorted through Soho, Picadilly, and South Kensington, but somehow skirted Covent Garden every time.

Finally I hit the cobblestone streets on the tip of Soho, and, with the help of other walkers, spotted the gray-and-white-striped awning of the boutique hotel.

FROM **Chris Huvane**
TO **Angie Banicki**
subject **Re: 30 before 30**

You have to go to the "Honor Bar" at the Covent Garden Hotel in London. SO cool. In Rome, you must see the Spanish Steps. Take a day trip down to Florence and run around and shop...but you must see Il Duomo, the most beautiful place in Europe if you ask me.

My eye caught on an empty, low-key bar to my right. I headed toward it, already knowing this was no honor bar but hoping the bartender could give me the truth. His head turned as he thought a moment, my anticipation rising. His eyebrows rose—

Then fell.

"Nope," he said. "But try the hotel's front desk. Maybe they can lead you in the right direction."

After walking through the Covent Garden's chic black doors, I walked straight to the check-in desk.

"Is there a bar here called the 'Honor Bar'?"

The girl at the desk looked at me like I was a pesky insect in her brightly colored garden. "Mmm, no, I don't really know what you're talking about."

Not willing to give up hope, I turned my attention to the chubby, pleasant-looking guy with glasses who was quietly tidying up next to her, pretending not to be interested.

"My friend Chris who works for GQ sent me all the way from Los Angeles to find the Honor Bar."

The name drop seemed to help, because Mr. Chubs perked up right away and turned to the girl at the guest check-in.

"I'll take care of it," he said with a tone of gravity and seriousness, then turned to me.

THE COVENT GARDEN HOTEL

FROM LONELY PLANET:

"SMACK IN THE HEART OF THEATRELAND, THIS HOSPITAL TURNED ROMANTIC BOUTIQUE HOTEL IS UNQUESTIONABLY ONE OF THE MOST CHARMING PLACES TO STAY IN LONDON— ONE OF DESIGNER KIT KEMP'S FINEST. THE 58 ROOMS ARE ALL DIFFERENT—DIFFERENT SIZES, COLORS, AND THEMES. THE PUBLIC SPACES ARE A MODERN VERSION OF THE CONTEMPORARY BRITISH SITTING ROOM."

"I'm Adam. Come with me. I'll explain the thing to you. We don't have an Honor Bar."

"What? Then where are we going?"

"What we have is the honesty bar. But it's not really a bar. It's within the hotel, a place where you get drinks."

"Perfect. So I can get a drink there!"

"No, you really can't have a drink there. But I'll show you."

We walked up the regal, winding staircase under the high ceilings—toward *what*, I still wasn't sure. I continued to explain that I would be happy to pay for a drink. In the *bar*.

He was walking us through a door marked LIBRARY.

"As I told you. No bar. These books and this room are for GUESTS ONLY."

Inside, it was stunning—a carved marble fireplace, shelves of beautiful books, soft couches, and chairs in a bright purple and yellow that somehow fit perfectly against the more stately oak walls.

Adam was now plainly enjoying being in charge of this riddle, his round little face like a Cheshire Cat.

He continued on, taking me to the far side of the room, sauntering as if it was his very own living room. Finally he pointed to what looked like a broom closet door. But sure enough, there are the magic words: HONESTY BAR, in painted lettering.

"This is the honesty bar." Adam's eyebrows rose as he paused for dramatic effect. I started to wonder if, when he opened the door, a body would fall out.

"Well, open the door already!" I laughed.

He swung open the door. No dead bodies, no boozing celebrities, no debauched dignitaries. No bartender or stools. Instead, only a little mini-kitchen with counters on each side. It looked like the kitchen of the tiniest NY studio, yet was stocked up like my Thanksgiving dinners in LA. One countertop held a big bucket of ice with a bottle of Grey Goose and a bottle of Dom, white wine, and rosé. The opposite side had a line of bottled liquor—every kind of alcohol you can imagine. At the end of the counter was a clipboard to log your booze. "Room 121 Angie Banicki one glass of Pinot noir," you'd write, and it'd be charged to your room bill. Then you'd pour yourself a glass of wine and watch the library fill up with characters. There was something about that library—it was the kind of place that made you want to do something naughty.

Honesty bars, I'd find out later, are something you'll find in many international hotels. But in the moment it all felt like a game of Clue played out in real life, and I was most excited by this new bit of knowledge.

Did Chris give me the wrong name on purpose or was he just so drunk that he didn't remember it right? He had been here doing a GQ shoot for Sherlock Holmes. Probably the latter, with the bill for everything picked up by the studio anyway, knowing Chris.

"Oh, do I have stories for you about the honesty bar! Come over here." Adam patted one of the big, fluffy corduroy couches. I had planned to try and charm my way into a drink but decided to play along instead. We sat down and Adam leaned in conspiratorially, as if tabloid reporters might be hiding under every couch. "Let me just tell you. I mean, we've had everyone here from Jack Nicholson to Liv Tyler. And some CRAZY things have happened within these walls. I could tell you if you promise not to…."

"Stop. Wait. No," I said, laughing and covering my ears. "This isn't a celebrity tell-all. I'm looking to be inspired."

Adam frowned.

"Inspired?"

He didn't get it.

"Some people sent me to restaurants. Some sent me to go look at their favorite famous places. For example, what is your favorite place in London? If someone were to ask you what inspires you in London, what would you tell them?"

He looked bewildered, then thoughtful. Finally his face seemed to light up.

"If inspired is what you're looking for…

He paused, a little unsure. I egged him on.

"Well: There's a pastry shop a few streets over, Coffee, Cake & Kink…"

I smiled encouragingly.

"…and they have the most unbelievable secret cheesecake… and cakes where you can choose your own frosting… and…"

He rattled off more details, losing his self-consciousness as the delicious memories inspired him.

"You've got to visit. It's magic!"

So I didn't get a drink at this bar—instead I got some honesty.

BIO ▼
CHRIS HUVANE

Chris and I are from the same tribe. We have 573 friends in common on Facebook. Like me, Chris comes from an Irish Catholic family, so he knows what truths are told in confessionals. He was the Senior West Coast editor of GQ for years before shifting into talent management at Management 360— an amazing career shift that speaks to Chris' ability to make it all happen. His clients are lucky to have him!

TRIPPING POINT

One man's David is another man's cheesecake. Find your thing and be true to it.

COFFEE CAKE & KINK

HAILED AS "THE BEST THING SINCE STRAP-ONS AND SLICED BREAD" COFFEE, CAKE & KINK IS WHERE COFFEE, CAKE, AND NAUGHTINESS COMBINE. ORIGINALLY A FUSION CAFE, DISHING OUT TREATS TOPPED OFF WITH EROTICA, SINCE THE CLOSURE OF ITS ORIGINAL PREMISES IN 2008 THE BAKERY HAS EVOLVED INTO A FULLY FLEDGED SOCIAL ENTERPRISE. THEY ARE CURRENTLY LOOKING FOR A NEW SPACE IN CENTRAL LONDON. FROM THEIR WEB SITE: "OUR UNDERSTAND-ING OF 'KINK' IS THAT OF ADVENTURE AND FUN. IT IS LIVING IN A UNIQUE WAY AND WALKING ONE'S OWN PATH IN LIFE, TRUTHFUL TO ONESELF AND OTHERS, AND BEING RESPECTED FOR THAT. THROUGH EV-ERYTHING WE DO, WHETH-ER IN A PHYSICAL SPACE, ONLINE, OR THROUGH OUR PROJECTS, WE PROVIDE A FRIENDLY, NON-JUDGMEN-TAL ENVIRONMENT FOR SELF-DISCOVERY AND THE ENJOYMENT AND CELEBRA-TION OF DIVERSITY AND CREATIVITY."

CHAPTER 7 FOR YOU DEAR, ANYTHING

DESTINATION Palace Theatre, London
INSPIRATION "Curb Your Enthusiasm's" Jeff Garlin's email sends me to a historical spot where he found magic—but getting in isn't easy.

● ● ● ● ● ● ● ● ● ● ● ● ● ● ● ● ● ●

My head was full of thoughts about the great funnyman Jeff Garlin, of "Curb Your Enthusiasm" fame, as I made my way to the West End, to the Palace Theatre. I had tried and failed to get tickets to see "SPA-MALOT" at the Palace, but that wasn't going to stop me from having my Jeff Garlin moment in the place where he had found his calling as a comedian. I was just going to have to do it without a ticket.

Time to get creative. Focus. It was time for Mission Jeff Garlin.

FROM **Jeff Garlin**
TO **Angie Banicki**
subject **No Subject**

Here is my answer lovely Angie. Please go to the Palace Theatre in London. I went about 15 years ago when I was all set to quit comedy. I was depressed and burnt out. Anyway I went to a show (OLIVER) at the palace theatre. During the show something happened to me. It was like a punch in the face. I realized that I was born to be a comedian. I actually started to cry.

I rode one of the famous red buses to the Palace Theatre in the West End. With its cobblestone central square and red brick façade, this place has been ground central for musical theatre in London all the way back to the 1880s. I had walked past the theatre at show time and seen it swarming with people. Now in mid-day, the square was nearly empty. I liked it this way—solid, stable, waiting in anticipation. You could feel it in the air surrounding the theater.

Out front, the box office was shut tight and marked CLOSED. This would require a more unorthodox entrance. I ever so sneakily sauntered over to the side door off the alley marked PRIVATE. It was very Oliver Twist, which seemed appropriate since that's what Jeff had seen in the theatre. As I approached the door, I switched into go mode and cruised through. Nothing could stop me. Inside, I found myself in a line with actors, backstage help, and backups. Everyone was in their heads, re-

THE PALACE THEATRE

"THE PALACE THEATRE IS A WEST END THEATRE IN THE CITY OF WESTMINSTER IN LONDON. ITS RED-BRICK FACADE DOMINATES THE WEST SIDE OF CAMBRIDGE CIRCUS NEAR THE INTERSECTION OF SHAFTESBURY AVENUE AND CHARING CROSS ROAD. RICHARD D'OYLY CARTE, PRODUCER OF THE GILBERT AND SULLIVAN OPERAS, COMMISSIONED THE THEATRE IN THE LATE 1880S TO BE A HOME OF ENGLISH GRAND OPERA. THE THEATRE OPENED AS THE 'ROYAL ENGLISH OPERA HOUSE' WITH ARTHUR SULLIVAN'S 'IVANHOE.' NO EXPENSE WAS SPARED TO GIVE THE SHOW 'EVERY IMAGINABLE EFFECT OF SCENIC SPLENDOUR.' IT RAN FOR 160 PERFORMANCES, BUT WHEN IT FINALLY CLOSED, CARTE HAD NO NEW WORK TO REPLACE IT, AND THE OPERA HOUSE HAD TO CLOSE AS WELL. IT WAS, ACCORDING TO CRITIC HERMAN KLEIN, 'THE STRANGEST COMMINGLING OF SUCCESS AND FAILURE EVER CHRONICLED IN THE HISTORY OF BRITISH LYRIC ENTERPRISE!' ULTIMATELY THE PALACE WOULD THRIVE, BUT CARTE HAD NO PART OF IT. WITHIN A YEAR OF 'IVANHOE' CLOSING, HE SOLD THE THEATRE AT A LOSS.
    —WIKIPEDIA

hearsing lines, and prepping, not seeming to take notice of the outsider. Good. But when I got up to the interior ticket window, the woman sitting there caught my eyes. I immediately knew she knew. The jig was up. So I talked fast.

"Listen, I just need to get in the theater for a picture, I leave tomorrow and this is my only chance…"

She shook her head at me. Whatever I was, she wasn't having a part of it.

"Honey, I'm not the one to help you. You need to try back in 30 minutes. Sorry."

I checked my watch. It was 4 p.m. The show didn't start until 6, so there was still time to make some moves. I tried to gather intel, but there was none here. On the plus side, everything felt very casual—therefore easily infiltrated.

I decided to check out the Coaches & Horses, a nearby watering hole for the theatre set. I quickly made friends with Joost, the skinny red-haired young bartender who was the opposite of the cliché for the profession—freckle-faced, almost shy, although he was a bartender to a T with his open ear and thoughtful advice. We didn't get very far, though—*4:30 already!*

I ran back to the theater. I got to the door and my intuition screamed at me. This wasn't going to happen—yet. Sure enough, I spoke to another woman who sent me away with a, "no." Yet another underling. I needed someone with power.

At this point, I considered giving up. No one so far had been remotely accommodating. I could barely get anyone even to listen to my story. But when someone you aspire to be like tells you they discovered their reason for living in this very spot, you do everything in your power to get there too, right? How could you not?

I recommitted.

BIO ►►

JEFF GARLIN

Jeff Garlin has a special place in my Midwestern heart. A Chicagoan with a big, booming, contagious laugh, just like my great Uncle Joe. I mean, Joe was more of a "pull my thumb" kinda guy, but he had the same big funny heart. Jeff treated my family like family—he spent time with my brother JJ, the actor, at one of my BlackBerry events. He gave JJ advice. Once you're in with one Banicki, you get us all. My favorite Jeff story is when I emailed a request to his publicist asking him to do an interview for a show I was working on for the Sundance Channel. I got a call within 10 minutes. "Ok, Angie. I'm in. I'll do the show. What do you need?" Jeff didn't even read the email before agreeing to it. Jeff isn't only a stand-up guy, actor, and producer, he's also written a book *My Footprint: Carrying the Weight of the World* is his hilarious account of his journey to lessen both his physical and carbon footprint. Finally, he's a connector, introducing me and many other Hollywood seekers to Nancy Cooke de Herrera, who introduced the Beatles to the Maharishi and gives one-on-one trainings in transcendental meditation in her Los Angeles home.

After killing more time with Joost, I went back. Now the square was filling up, since it was much closer to show time. This was it. I had to make it happen. The woman who I spoke to seemed to get that. She looked me up and down and said, "Okay, just stand right here. I'm gonna get someone. I don't think we can actually bring you into the theatre but we'll bring you into the front part."

That wasn't going to cut it, of course, but it was a step in the right direction. I'd figure it out.

She came back with one of the theatre managers—finally! I eyeballed him. There was nothing I could see to help me read how he'd react to my request. He was nondescript and unremarkable. His eyes and expression were neutral. I explained my story to him—my trip, Jeff Garlin, life changing moments, yadda yadda. My words hung in the air, as he stood there considering whether to give me a victorious third act.

We stared each other down, his poker face against my hopeful smile.

"OK, I think I can help you."

Cymbals strike and the big orchestra begins to play. In my head, anyway. It's happening!

Now we were both big smiles. Despite what the woman had said about keeping me in the lobby, he took me straight into the theatre.

"Which seat?"

As I eased into the seat where Jeff had sat, so many years back, I felt like I could make anything happen. The manager, now completely immersed in the Angie show, offered to snap pictures. I was still mugging for the camera when the audience began filing in.

TRIPPING POINT

Fortune favors the sneaky, or maybe just those with a genuine drive to live like their heroes.

CHAPTER 8 TEE TIME ON PAR IN LONDON

DESTINATION Navajo Joe, London

INSPIRATION Luke Donald, PGA golfer and college friend, shows me another side of London.

● ● ● ● ● ● ● ● ● ● ● ● ● ● ● ● ● ● ●

Sitting cross-legged on a dirty, dusty college frat house floor, throwing ping-pong balls into cups of beer is my favorite memory with Luke Donald. That guy is an intense competitor. As we played our game of Cups, Luke got more serious. I remember finding a magazine with Tiger Woods on the cover and putting it behind the cups in hopes of distracting Luke. It only pushed him to do better—he beat Tiger's low strokc avcrage one year while we were at college. Can I take some credit for that?

When I arrived in London, I was thrilled to find out Luke would be there too—but only overlapping two nights with me. I was immediately on it, determined to hang out together while we were there. Luke was game but a little disappointed that I was more interested in visiting with him then re-enacting the beautiful date night with his wife that he had described in his travel moment email to me.

Like it or not, Luke Donald was going to be my Luke Donald moment.

That evening started with a friend at a restaurant called Hakkasan, recommended to me by another friend, director Frank E. Flowers. To get to the restaurant, you have to walk down a small, dark street. At the end, a guy in a trench coat checks for your reservation before letting you inside, down a long, plain staircase into the subterranean restaurant. Blue lights and lattice walls, very dramatic. It was a great meal, and we sampled all the fun drinks before heading to meet Luke and his high school buddies for karaoke.

Our karaoke experience in London was kind of like that Cups memory I have—dusty, boozy, and fun. Vodka tonics all around in the basement bar of a converted warehouse. Luke's high school buds had a similar gentle kindness as Luke's, setting us at ease even before the drinks did.

It was fun to watch Luke in his element. His accent got a little stronger, his mannerisms more defined. He and his friends went full-on goofball, doing a group number.

Ultimately, we closed out the place. Clothes on, of course.

LUKE DONALD

The funny thing about the world-renowned pro-golfer Luke Donald is that he's shy and quiet. He was that way at Northwestern, where he studied art theory, and he still is now that he's held the title of World Number One. (He held it for 55 weeks!) In fact, the night we spent together in London was the most extroverted I've ever seen him. Luke's ability to live his passions—his golf career, his family life, his interest in food and wine—while remaining down-to-earth and available to old friends inspires me enormously.

THE HISTORY OF KARAOKE

"THE WORD KARAOKE COMES FROM *KARA*, EMPTY (AS IN KA-RATE—EMPTY HAND) AND OKE (SHORT FOR *OKESUTORA*), ORCHESTRA. WHILE MOST PEOPLE AGREE THAT IT STARTED IN KOBE, JAPAN, THE ORIGINS OF KARAOKE ARE OBSCURE. ONE STORY CLAIMS THAT A SNACK BAR OWNER, WHEN A PERFORMER FAILED TO APPEAR, PUT ON TAPES OF MUSIC AND ASKED PEOPLE IF THEY WANTED TO SING. FROM SUCH INSIGNIFICANT BEGINNINGS, KARAOKE HAS SPREAD, NOT JUST THROUGHOUT JAPAN, BUT ALSO THROUGHOUT THE WORLD, AND THE TERM KARAOKE—WHILE PRONOUNCED DIFFERENTLY—HAS BEEN ACCEPTED INTO COMMON LANGUAGE USAGE. —FROM ESSORTMENT.COM'S "HISTORY OF KARAOKE"

Here was one of my favorite days out in London:

While planning a night out with some friends, I decided to go all out and spend a night in London at the famous Mandarin Oriental in Hyde Park in Knightsbridge. The rooms are classical and elegant, and although the hotel is far from cheap (not sure that you can find anything cheap in London!) the location is one of the best there is.

After a lazy morning, my wife and I crossed the busy Knightsbridge street, and ducked under Harvey Nichols to a little restaurant called Wagamama's - a far from chic place, where the seating is communal along benches. The staff are friendly though and the food is great, specializing in Japanese noodles and soups - a great little place to meet up for a casual lunch with friends, before embarking on some serious shopping.

That night, after a little nap to get ready for the evening's festivities, we got all dressed up. London is all about looking sharp, and making an effort, somewhat like New York, so it's a good idea to bring some of your best outfits. After waiting for my wife to finish glamming up, we went downstairs to the hotel bar to meet up with our friends. The bar is a very chic and cozy little spot. Make sure to go early if you want to get a seat.

After a couple of cocktails, we headed over to Zuma, a 5-minute walk away. Zuma again is very trendy, and usually has some paparazzi outside, just waiting for the many celebs that like to go there. Zuma is very much like Japonais in Chicago, an Asian style restaurant where the food is best shared and enjoyed together. It's all good on the menu, you really can't go wrong. As we were a large group we had one of the back tables, where you sit on little cushions with your shoes off, which in hindsight was probably a little too private, as it was a little away from the hustle and bustle of the main dining room. I strongly recommend the mojitos; they're delicious and really easy to drink. After a few of these, the night will take care of itself......

Hope that helps!

Luke

TRIPPING POINT

Karaoke is the world's universal language.

CHAPTER 9 A DAY AT 30 ROCK

DESTINATION Basement bathroom of The Citadines Apart'Hotel, Gloucester Road, South Kensington, London

INSPIRATION Jack McBrayer, a.k.a. "30 Rock"'s Kenneth, inspires me to rely on the kindness of strangers. The result is more of a Liz Lemon moment.

• • • • • • • • • • • • • • • • • • • •

And the page turned.

The day that ended as my Jack McBrayer moment started out feeling like it was inspired by Liz Lemon, "30 Rock"'s disaster-a-moment writer heroine. I started writing comedy, but only when the writing ceased did the real episode begin.

Dressed for a run but not ready to exercise, I found myself sitting at Starbucks with a mug full of ginger tea and a head full of words. I picked up that unit which is rarely far from my hand—my BlackBerry—and my fingers went into overdrive. I couldn't stop them if I tried as they furiously typed out descriptions of the new cast of characters who had entered my life in London. I was tearing up and laughing (snort) as I released the jumble from my head on to that small screen.

In just 30 minutes, my whole story unfolded beautifully. It was genius, obviously. I felt elated and enlightened. I was funny, really funny. It was time to email the masterpiece to a lucky recipient. Jack Donaghy, you'd be offering me a show, it was that good. (Snort.)

Then the coffee shop turned from sunny bright to gloomy gray.

Jaw drop. It was gone, pages and pages. Those words went from my head to my BlackBerry to…Blackblurry. My head's blurry. The email had disappeared.

I lost control of my head, my body, and my awareness of common social behavior. I began frantically pressing buttons, holding keys, scrolling up and down, but there was no trace. Then came the hair pulling, eye squinting, face rubbing, and feet stomping.

FROM   Jack McBrayer
TO   Angie Banicki
subject **Europe Trip**

I want to help you out with your trip to Europe, but I'm afraid I'm not as well traveled as a lot of your other friends are. I spent a semester in England in college, and that was great fun. I was on work-study, so I had to work my job (building maintenance) on the weekends while all the other kids got to travel around. Although I didn't get around as much as some of the others, I did have a wonderful time.

One thing that I took away from my time there was a true enjoyment and appreciation of the people I was around. My host family, the English professors, my co-workers in the manor (we studied in a manor!)...All of those guys really shaped my time there and made it very meaningful.

So, I guess my contribution would be this: get to know a couple of the locals in whatever city/country you stay in. Invite them out to dinner and get a real taste of how citizens of that place are. You know they'll have great stories and strong opinions and will be otherwise...very interesting.

Is this anything that you're looking for? I wish I had a tip like, "try this Indian restaurant in London's West End", but I don't have anything like that.

Anyway, have a fun trip, and be safe. Give me a holler if you need anything, and otherwise, enjoy yourself! And happy birthday.

Jackie McB

Like someone was squeezing me, my face scrunched up and tears poured out.

I had one moment of brilliance. One hour. And the universe stole it. Sniffle. Sniffle. I would be okay. Big breath.

And then, more uncontrollable sobbing. Liz Lemon, this had to feel worse than you felt after Jon Hamm walked in on you pooping.

Pushing and pulling and pushing, I finally shoved through the door of Starbucks.

I ran out, a very uncomfortable exit with legs tripping, arms flailing, mascara from the night before smeared on my cheeks. Social behavioral skills still not back.

Get home to my hotel. Do what you know works. Go on a run.

By the time I had my tennies on at the hotel, I had already called my mother and gotten some reassuring words that I rejected out of hand, but secretly they made me feel a little better. My social skills and behavioral awareness were returning. I'd run the rest out. But first I'd stop by the front desk to see if I could extend my stay one more night.

An incredibly tightpants snobby receptionist blinked at my freshly washed, but surely red-eyed face.

"The rate will return to our standard rate and I will need to know immediately so I can sort it. By the way, if you are leaving you'll need to be checked out in 30 minutes. 12 p.m., noon."

Every sentence ended with a pointed snobbish poke in a pitch two octaves higher than my own.

My lower lip quivered as I headed back to my room, but I felt resolve bubbling up in me. I knew what I had to do. I had to get out of this hotel, fast. I'd show that snob. It was time to take Jack McBrayer's advice and call upon the kindness of locals. I hatched my plan while manically shoving gummy bears into my mouth. Did I mention I stress eat like Liz Lemon? First things first. Slowly release the gummy...

I called sweet Ann, my new friend from a fabulous night in London that didn't make it into the book. She understood immediately.

"Check yourself out and we'll figure it out."

I breathed a sigh of relief—just for a moment.

Time to pack. I immediately started cramming clothes into my suitcase and backpack. It was like the Tasmanian Devil had hit my room and then did another run through.

Back at the front desk at 12:17 p.m.

You didn't really think I'd check out precisely when snot-nose told me to, did you?

Outside the hotel, the weather in London was hot, uncharacteristically warm, and sunny for London, just like my first day had been. Nevertheless, I decided it wasn't a bad idea to get a workout in so I started walking toward Ann's in Kensington...yes, a 4-mile trek from Soho. I had only time on my side since Ann wouldn't be home till 6 p.m., and I wasn't ready to be around people after my trauma of the morning.

Scene: The Walk. Monologue inside my head:

1:04 p.m. It is actually really hot today in London. (I start to sweat.)

1:06 p.m. Sweat through it. What else are you gonna do, write? (Teardrop.) I'd prefer a lemon drop.

1:26 p.m. Are you really pulling luggage while walking across London? Through Soho Square?! You've lost it.

1:46 p.m. This isn't a workout. This is pain. I see the Thames River.

1:50 p.m. Do you really think this 15 pounds is going to change your life? 15 pounds, that is, in British coin for a cab. Come on!

2:01 p.m. You've probably gone 17 blocks and this is a waste of everyone's time. Get in a cab. Moron.

2:04 p.m. (Sweaty, sore and stumbling downhill.) "CABBIE! South Kensington, please." (Deep breath.) Liz Lemon, no more punishing yourself.

We pulled up to Ann's apartment. I paid my cabbie and entered the Citadines.

I had no key. No plan. But I had made it. As I walked toward the front desk, I focused for a second on how my day might go. My short conversation with Ann was that she'd be home to let me in around 6. Meanwhile, in my frazzled state, I'd made a 6 p.m. pub date and told another friend we could meet at 8. I also told Ann I was taking her to dinner for letting me crash. My London season finale was going to be full of surprises—for everyone.

The woman at the front desk had no idea what she was in for.

"Hi there. Can I help you?"

She's blond, meek, and English is definitely not her first language.

Sweet as can be, I start to explain my situation, that I am staying with Ann, but need a key.

"I'm sorry, I cannot help you. No key. No tenant. No room."

She's like Cerie, the blond writer's assistant on "30 Rock." But again, I'm reading a dead end.

"Wait. Let me explain it to you..." Before I can go into Angie pitch mode, Cerie interrupts and says she's going to get her manager. I can

71

feel it. I'm a "special case."

I felt confident as a chubby, friendly-faced manager walked toward me. He was definitely no tightpants and I'd had some time to think about my case. Here was my Kenneth, my page at the Citadines. Sweet, sweet Kenneth.

"Hi there." My approach is meek and adoring.

"I'm sorry, I just don't think I can help you."

"Before you tell me no, let me explain. I don't need you to call Ann, or give me a key to her place. Maybe you can just let me into her room. I need a shower, a bathroom, and a place to throw my luggage."

"OK ma'am, well I..."

"No 'ma'am's, silly. I'm young!" I flirt.

The back and forth continues and I squeeze his plump arm. He relents.

"OK, OK. Here's what we can do—I've got a place to keep your luggage. In terms of a shower or bathroom, I just cannot promise. I simply can't let you in Ann's room."

Timing is everything. I nodded, thanked him profusely, and put my luggage in the storage spot. I threw in a hug as an afterthought, to help the case later.

I exited the hotel and set out to traverse Kensington. Hot air devoured me again but at least now I was light-weight and luggage free.

A good run, even a speed walk, always resets me. Sweat is so much better than tears.

I explored the flower gardens of Kensington and the flats adorned with moms pushing strollers and young men walking dogs.

Back to Citadines. I now had 30 minutes before I needed to be in Soho looking pretty. I had to get this done.

I find my Kenneth, Mr. Chubby Sweetface, and once more make my plea. I leave nothing on the table.

"I just need to wash up so I can make it over to meet people on my last night in London. I will do anything for a shower. I don't even need a room. Just running water." My Kenneth is trying to stand his ground, but I feel him teetering. "It's so important for my journey. You will become part of my inspiration. Pleeeeease."

He rubs his temple and looks to the side. He is breaking!

"Well there's one…"

"Yes!" He looks at me in shock when I jump at the offer before he's said it.

"Shower?...Yes!" I say with a big smile to his questioning eyes. Best to define my enthusiasm—shower, clean—in case he thinks I will agree to something dirty.

"It's our staff bathroom in the basement. Not used often, so, well, might not be very nice. I will get you towels and supplies."

"Thank you thank you THANK YOU. Yes. Great. Let me grab what I need out of my luggage."

Cue the comedic montage music.

My Kenneth, now my second kind local, took his keys and carried my bag as we descended together into a dingy basement. We passed employees who looked at me in horror as I waited for Kenneth to grab the key to the bathroom. I was too focused on time and my night ahead to notice how disgusting it all was.

The bathroom door opened and the smell of some strange mildew wafted out. This was Europe it might have been centuries old. I took a deep breath through my mouth and entered.

I tossed one towel on the ground and placed my dress on top. I'm not a clean freak and have no problem walking around the gym bath-room bare foot, but this was bad. I pulled out my flip-flops and ripped off my clothes, only to realize that another surprise had arrived right on time, though I had completely lost track. Ahhh….My dramatic crying fit of the morning now made sense.

I twisted and tugged on a faucet that was mostly rusted shut.

Finally it creaked on, choking and sputtering, fighting to push the water out. It wasn't very hot, but it was water and soap, and that was all that was needed. In no time I was finally CLEAN! I breathed in the lemony fresh smell and spent a full five seconds feeling relieved and renewed.

With a big night ahead—beer at the pub, possible date, and last night out in London—I must look cute, and in record time. I jumped out, threw on my long cotton green dress, ran a brush through wet hair, then dabbled on moisturizer and blush.

Time spent in dreary bathroom: Under 10 minutes.

I threw open the door for my final touches and the big reveal. My Kenneth, waiting right by the door, was visibly shocked at my transformation. I guess my puckered lemon face had finally turned into a smile, and my vanilla apricot perfume had overpowered the basement's stench, making everyone happy.

I hugged Kenneth as he helped me throw my stuff together before we headed back up. "You are so kind to wait for me. I will call Ann and let her know I'm headed out and that you are keeping my luggage down here!"

Kenneth stood just a little taller, proud of himself for his good deed and basking in my graciousness. When you ask for help and get it, that person usually gets just as much pleasure from helping as you do from the help. Good pitch.

As for "local" Ann, what started as someone offering me a roof for a night turned into a friend for life. I'd build a roof for her if she needed one.

BIO ▶▶

JACK McBRAYER

Kenneth Ellen Parcell, a.k.a. Kenneth the Page, is a character on "30 Rock." According to *Wikipedia*, "Kenneth is a perpetually cheerful page. An awkward yet polite rube, he is always smiling, excited, and happy to do his menial job." The man who plays him, Jack McBrayer, is no rube—but he is just as gracious and kind as the character he plays. When Jack's career was first taking off, I often hooked him up with freebies from companies I was working with. Without fail, he would take a picture of himself with, say, his new Ugg boots, and send it along with a personalized thank you note. I loved that.

TRIPPING POINT

When you get lemoned, and it will happen in travel, make a lemon drop.

CHAPTER 10 SHAKEN NOT STIRRED

DESTINATION Dukes Bar on St James Place, London

INSPIRATION Matthew Rhys of "Brothers & Sisters" gave me clear direction on what I MUST DO in London—which turns out to involve a very stiff drink and, as Moneypenny would say, "a cunning linguist."

● ● ● ● ● ● ● ● ● ● ● ● ● ● ● ● ● ●

Finding Dukes Bar on my last day in London became my very own James Bond mission. After being dropped at two wrong hotels and given a slew of bad directions from locals, I found myself taking a deep breath as I walked up to the unmarked spot at the end of a residential street. Please be the place. I was 45 minutes late and in panic mode. Fortunately Angie Panicki has one thing going for her—she makes friends fast. Probably because we are at our most honest when we're feeling completely off-kilter.

Or is that just me?

Oversized armoire chairs sat just inside the entrance, and a small, intimate bar was just to the right. As I walked toward it, I felt like I was in the living room of a charming castle. Down past the bar I spotted a boyishly handsome, dark-haired man in a suit who I desperately hoped was the "friend" my brother had sent me to meet—particularly since there wasn't anyone else in the bar under 60.

As I walked up, he gave me a big, gorgeous grin, setting down his martini to jump up and pull me into a hug. It was as if he was my own brother, and I immediately felt all the frustration of trying to get to the bar fade. And straight out of an episode of "I Love Lucy," I couldn't stop myself from diving right in, complete with blurting and blabbering, "Oh My God—You are not going to believe what happened to me!!

Chris, no one knows where anything is in London, and trying to find you was a nightmare scavenger hunt with trick directions...and then there was the 'fake' St Dukes bathroom...."

Chris was laughing as he pulled me down into the comfy armchair across from him. The move didn't stop me as I rattled on about the comedy of errors that ensued en route to our meeting. Mid-rambling, I came up for air just in time to throw a little blame his way. "But WAIT! You?! You didn't confirm our drinks!"

We both laughed, realizing that I hadn't even waited for a, "hello, nice to meet you" before I was calling him out like he really was my brother. Chris seemed entertained and possibly a bit overwhelmed.

"The bartenders thought I was lying about a girl coming to meet me!"

We laughed again.

"Well here we are, and I need a drink!"

I looked back toward the bar and took in the atmosphere. Dukes liquors up a sophisticated crowd. All the men were smoking cigars and wearing padded elbow jackets.

Our waiter, an adorable little 70-year-old, approached, as if on cue. "Well, hello young lady! What can I get you?"

FROM **Matthew Rhys**
TO **Angie Banicki**
subject **Re: Palms Place Opening - LAS VEGAS INVITE**

Here's the quick list...
Have a pint at the 'Coach and Horses' Greek Street, in Soho. It's a bit of a dive and soon to close. It was Peter O'Toole's favourite pub as well as Oliver Reed. Very famous with the old brigade of actors.

Around the corner is Kettners restaurant (very reasonable) - Oscar Wilde used to eat there. Still retains old school charm and has a pianist and great Champagne bar.

Stand on Waterloo bridge at night and look in both directions. (Embankment tube station. Green line.) Def do this one.

Go to Borough market on Sunday morning. (Check it's open). It's on the northern line (underground). (The Black line).

Go to Primrose Hill. Have lunch at the Engineer pub and then walk to the top of the hill and look out over London.

Walk to the top of Hampstead Heath and look out over London. (Close to Primrose Hill).

Go to Columbia Road flower market on a Sunday morning.

Have a cocktail at the Hilton hotel Hyde Park. 17th floor, look out over London.

This one you MUST do - go to Dukes Hotel on St. James Place off St. James St. and order a martini. It's a thing of beauty.

"This is a really special moment," I announced dramatically. "We have been sent to order the Ian Fleming martini!" Something about being in this bar where the medium age was 73 with my surrogate brother was making me my silliest, most unguarded self.

Mr. Belvedere—that's what I'll call our waiter man—laughed at my determination.

"Are you sure? It's quite strong."

My eyes lit up. "Well, I don't have a choice. Bring it out. I've been sent to taste it." I made it clear I was excited for the challenge.

Mr. Belvedere grinned and said with a smile, "Do you know who created that drink?"

I looked at Chris and shrugged. "Ian Fleming, I'd guess?"

"Me! I did!" Mr. Belvedere grinned even wider and puffed out his chest.

"Before the first James Bond movie was ever made, Ian would come in and have this drink. He would come and write. This was his favorite place. We will actually make the drink in front of you."

I clapped my hands as Mr. Belvedere turned to get what he needed for the drinks. Chris and I looked at each other and laughed, curious to see what Mr. Belvedere would do next. Chris shook his head.

"Who are you? You've already made a friend in that old man."

The comment made me realize that, traveling alone, I was getting used to all these magical mini-adventures. They were my new normal. It takes a traveler to rediscover that something as silly as having a drink prepared in front of you can be a revelation if you open yourself to it. I mean, I might always enjoy something like that—but it's doubly fun when you're not holding anything back.

Chris and I tried to guess how strong our drinks would be. We were like two teenagers waiting to try our first sips of alcohol.

"You still haven't finished the story of your OMG day, Angie Banicki, and I believe you started another story in between about last night."

My brother once wrote an essay about me called, "Oh My God. You're not going to believe this!" Fine, so I say that a lot. But my life is an OMG, or I live in a constant state of feeling that way. And now, on a whirlwind adventure, it would seem that an unending stream of OMGs should finally be perfectly understandable and appropriate.

"You definitely don't know me yet," I warned Chris. "I'll finish all of those and start four more before we finish our first martinis."

Mr. Belvedere walked up rolling a cart filled with supplies and described the process for making the Ian Fleming special. He basked in all the attention we were giving him. It seemed he hadn't been asked about the Ian in quite some time, so he took his time explaining. The drink, with a wicked amount of vodka, was poured into the classic silver vessel and then "shaken, not stirred."

Mr. Belvedere's warm eyes fed off our giddy interest as he described the martini. I pulled out my camera to photograph our new friend as he performed his mixology—not that he would have called it that back at the dawn of Bond in the '50s. But he was clearly ahead of his time.

"No photos allowed in the establishment. I'm sorry," he said, noticing the camera.

"Oh please, please, you have to let me."

When the posterity of my journey is at stake, I am not above begging.

He shook his head no, but I saw him looking around. He was wavering, and I knew it was my cue.

"Please…. I promise, you can even have photo approval and I'll put it away after."

He paused and looked at me, still considering—I was almost there.

"I want to take a picture of you! You are famous! We can make sure no one else is nearby and it will just be captioned, 'the man who made the martini!'"

The switch flipped: "Me? The pretty girl really wants a picture of me?" He stood up straighter, smiling big and holding a cute, old man pose.

"Wait. But oh, I am old. Do I look okay?"

After one snap, the younger bartender sauntered over to bring lemon twists.

"Ooh, let's get one of the two of you too!"

His face fell.

"Oh no. He is much handsomer. The old man will get cut from the photo."

My affection for the man surged. He was genuinely concerned he would be forgotten. I took care to remind him he was the Ian Fleming martini's creator and true star here.

Mr. Belvedere smiled one more time for the camera, satisfied, then left us to sample our drinks. The martini was like nothing I'd ever tasted, although I did have flashbacks to the first few times I'd taken shots in college. The Ian Fleming is a drink that says, "I want to get right to it. Hit me with your best shot."

I felt the drink heat up my insides—adding to the warmth generated by the conversation and the moment. The handsome Chris and I went on to have an evening to remember—but that's an "OMG!" that I'll keep to myself.

BIO ▶▶

MATTHEW RHYS

Matthew Rhys gets a gold star not just for being one of the most social guys in Hollywood, but for being one of the nicest. He could have a beer with any person in the world and they would love him—he's a Welsh everyman who once wanted to be a farmer. In Hollywood, he ignored people's warnings that he'd be typecast if he took the role of a gay lawyer on ABC's prime-time drama "Brothers & Sisters." It turned out to be a great move—the role won him fans and acclaim, and now he's been cast in the lead opposite Keri Russell on "The Americans."

TRIPPING POINT

A martini is a thing of beauty.

QUICK HITS | LONDON

CHRIS HARRISON | "HOST, THE BACHELOR"

…My favorite part of London is High Street Kensington. We found this **wonderful little jewelry store tucked away just a block above Kensington St.** Her name is Kirsten Goss and she's very talented…

• •

AMY ELMER | DREAMWORKS

…You have to do like the Brits and **go to a pub right after work gets out** (4-5, 6ish). Hordes of people hang out and usually everyone is really friendly. Try the Westbourne Tavern in Notting Hill…

• •

ROMANY MALCO | ACTOR, "WEEDS"

…I went to the projects in London around midnight with a girl I was dating and we smoked a joint on the roof of London's tallest project building. **All you could hear was the wind, gunshots and sirens.** It's a fond memory that I would not want you to experience under any circumstances…

• •

CHARLEY WALTERS

…I went on this crazy tour called **the Jack the Ripper walk**. It is so interesting and kind of creepy, too—not in a fear-for-your-life kind of way, but in a makes-you-think way….

• •

LYDIA HEARST

…Do tea time at the Wallace Collection…

• •

DAVID ARQUETTE | ACTOR

…Aspinall's is a private gambling club. Classic spot. A member has to introduce you…

• •

JASON REITMAN | DIRECTOR, "UP IN THE AIR", "JUNO"

…When I was 25, I landed in London on the way to Prague. I was going for a film festival and only realized during my stopover in Heathrow that the Czechs had a visa requirement for Canadians. Thus began a 24-hour journey, pin-balling back and forth as I picked up documents, took photos, secured a new passport and applied for a visa. Towards the end of all this madness, I found myself outside the Canada House in Trafalgar Square waiting for my passport to dry. Next to me was the National Gallery, housing hundreds of years of the most important art in the world. While done briskly, my 45-minute tour of art history is one of my fondest traveling memories. Particularly Ruben's "Samson and Delilah"–**one of the most heartbreakingly beautiful paintings I've ever witnessed with my own eyes…**

• •

JAMES VALENTINE | SINGER, MAROON 5

…Most of my favorite memories are linked to the music venues we have played. Go try and see a show. Music is such a big part of the culture there, I think it would be appropriate. **My favorite venues are The Astoria, Brixton Academy, and Shepard's Bush Empire.** There is a little dingy club called Barfly in Camden where we played our first London show…I jog everywhere and love doing it in London in Hyde Park…

• •

TAYLOR MOMSEN | "GOSSIP GIRL"

…The most memorable person I met was **the Queen of England**. i got to present her with flowers at the premier of the Grinch. idk, maybe you have some hookup and can meet her, cus it was really cool…

• •

CAMILLE GUATY | "THE NINE"

…I'm challenging you to go to the palace and **seek out the palace guard who mysteriously stuck his tongue out at me**. I'm hoping you have a similar experience, so you can share it with others as I have. Just a hint…I think the key is not to try and make sure no one is around…

• •

AJ DIPERSIA | ACTOR
…London is all about booze…

• •

QUICK HITS | LONDON

JJ BANICKI | BROTHER

...Let the Brits do all the talking, they sound so charming. **Anything bright red is worth taking a picture next to**. Take a stroll through Kensington Park. Oh, and mind the gap....

• •

BEN LYONS | CORRESPONDENT, "EXTRA"

....A great London memory I had was **watching the sunrise from the Thames bridge right by the London eye and parliament and Big Ben**. Take a lap around the river, across the big new fancy bridge, and the old historic one. I did that with a chick and it was incredibly romantic....

• •

MILO VENTIMIGLIA | ACTOR, HEROES

...When I was 22 and in London, I knew nothing. **I let myself get caught up with the streets that were flooded with people** and just kinda moved to and fro with them. At night I'd go to the clubs I'd hear about during the day. And during the day I'd go to the cultural places I'd hear about at night....

• •

ALI PULITI | US WEEKLY

...You have to take the bus tour, that way you can see the entire city in the shortest time possible and then decide where you want to go...**Take the tube to Abbey Road** where you have to walk across the path like a Beatle and have someone take your picture....

• •

KRIS CAMPBELL

...Visit the Tower of London. One of my favorite travel moments was when as a kid, I posed for a picture with the taller-than-me teddy bear in a Beefeater uniform that guarded the entrance...

• •

Paris

CHAPTER 11 ANGIE IN WONDERLAND

DESTINATION The Eiffel Tower and Beyond

INSPIRATION Amaury Nolasco hooks me up with a new best friend, and G. Love sends us both tickets to his show in Paris.

• • • • • • • • • • • • • • • • • • • •

IF YOU DON'T KNOW WHERE YOU ARE GOING, ANY ROAD WILL GET YOU THERE.

–Lewis Carroll, Author, *Alice in Wonderland*

As a kid, Paris to me was the miniature copper Eiffel Tower perched on my parent's dining room showcase. I daydreamed of visiting the magical city as I stared at it and let my mind wander—strolling down the city streets filled with romanticized Parisians speaking in strong, sensual tones, and living a lifestyle I could only fantasize about through French photos in school.

In sixth grade, I chose France to report on for my country presentation. In order to make sure everyone in class loved Paris as much as I did, I went to overachiever level. Mom Banicki helped me make the famous French pastry profiteroles, better known in the U.S. as cream puffs. I brought them for the class to sample while I read to them about Paris. Afterward, I demonstrated how to make the delicacy with the puff-filler contraption. Squirting whipped cream and powdered sugar always wins classmates' votes.

My fall through the rabbit hole of London into my Paris wonderland happened by way of speed train the morning of my eighth day—which also happened to be the first day spent with a hangover, only slightly stunted by my boss Lara Shriftman's travel trip: "Make sure you get

Berocca! Best cure for a hangover."

I had read the ingredients and usage instructions while thinking in Alice terms. Eat me. Drink me. I almost just chewed the Berocca, a large, Alka-Seltzer-like tablet, but instead stopped myself and followed the directions, tossing it into a bottle of water and chugging.

I can appreciate a hangover as a reminder that I'm not superhuman. I especially don't mind the hangover during travel. A train ride with a little hangover helps avoid the fidgets.

It's the forced relax that I hate.

Jim, a Midwestern college grad traveler sitting next to me, provided me with a whiskey, which can also do the trick. In addition to the drink, Jim prepped me for my arrival into foreign land. He was the caterpillar to my Alice—with whiskey and advice replacing the mushrooms.

By the time I arrived in Paris, I knew what I wanted to do: Get myself to the Eiffel Tower as quickly as possible.

The trouble was, this was France. They all spoke French. I quickly discovered that I had left my college French back at college. After stumbling around the train station, I found someone who understood me enough to point toward a bus. Rushing to catch it in the sweltering heat, I looked up at the driver and realized I had no idea what to do. I nearly burst into tears.

He saw the swell and nodded for me to go ahead, telling me in broken English that he'd help with the ticket before I left. I slid between two patrons, grabbing onto the pole above us. The smell wasn't romantic or sensual, it was just strong, B.O. and French cheese. I held my breath, avoiding eye contact with the people crammed against me, and thought about French pastries and vanilla pudding instead.

As we pulled up to the Eiffel Tower, I stepped off the bus onto the sidewalk, holding my luggage, looking up at the beautiful mini copper statue grown to life—and bigger than I imagined.

FROM   **Amaury Nolasco**
TO   **Angie Banicki**
subject **30 Before 30**

1) Paris has to be the most amazing city in the world. I love NY, but Paris has an energy and feel to it that it's impossible to express in words. You just have to be there and you'll get what I'm saying. If you are into museums and seeing art then this is perfect for you. Me, on the other hand, I hate those places. I find them boring. I would tell you to go dining and walk and walk, and walk. Get away from the touristy areas.

A place that I loved, it's called Montmartre. There is an amazing church there, but besides that, there are all this little cafés, and bars where you can just sit down and watch the people pass you by and experience the life Parisians do. It's an old area of Paris. Lots of History. Cobble Stone streets. A lot of artists live there.

2) I loved St. Germain, It's the equivalent to SoHo in NY. Great place to meet people.

3) Hotel Costes, it's a hot hotel. Expensive, but a lot of good-looking people. The place to hang out, not to stay.

One of my favorite lounges, is called Milliodare. Fun, fun, fun..

xoxo

Amaury

    I took a deep breath. This was really Paris! At least, I thought it was. The Alice in me couldn't really be sure, but she was still delighted. The heat still lingered, but now I could inhale deeply, taking in the fresh air and wafts of cotton candy. The foreign voices that had seemed so harsh in the train station now sounded like music.

    I reluctantly turned away, preparing to drag my luggage to the near-by café my future host Jen had suggested as a place where we could meet. Café Champ de Mars would do to begin my mad tea party. I felt weak as a dormouse as I collapsed in a chair, pulled off my sweatshirt, threw down my luggage, and took a deep breath. Two minutes. No waiter. Leaving my bags—I'd rather them be stolen than have to pick them up one more time—I ventured inside where I found a waiter who laughed when I immediately pleaded for rosé.

Ten minutes later—maybe more—the waiter walked outside with my glass of wine. I was already learning that the French don't really care if you're in a hurry or not. Europeans in general operate on their own time, but in France, their apathy is legendary.

I was incredibly excited to sip that rosé. My waiter laughed as I gulped. He pointed to the menu with questioning eyes: Don't you want to eat something? I knew I should, but after the sweaty bus ride, I just wanted that cool cotton candy breeze and pink wine—my Paris fantasy.

Taking out my pink highlighted Paris journal, I decided to pick out all the places I'd go while pretending to be sophisticated and European in Paris. Soon I had attracted an older French man who, seeing I

THE EIFFEL TOWER

THE EIFFEL TOWER, NAMED AFTER ITS ENGINEER, GUSTAVE EIFFEL, IS AN IRON LATTICE TOWER LOCATED ON THE CHAMP DE MARS IN PARIS. ERECTED IN 1889, THE TOWER REMAINED THE HIGHEST STRUCTURE ON THE PLANET FOR OVER 40 YEARS UNTIL THE ARRIVAL OF THE CHRYSLER BUILDING. TODAY, IT IS STILL THE MOST-VISITED PAID MONUMENT IN THE WORLD, WITH OVER 7 MILLION PEOPLE ASCENDING IN 2011. WHILE IT MAY TODAY BE THE WORLD'S MOST RECOGNIZABLE SYMBOL OF URBAN SOPHISTICATION, AT THE TIME OF ITS CONSTRUCTION, FRENCH INTELLECTUALS AND ARTISTS SIGNED A PETITION AGAINST THIS "ODIOUS COLUMN OF BOLTED METAL."

was American, decided he would tell me where I should go in France. He would take me places. I tried to explain my journal but his English was then gone and so were his manners. He was the first of many disappointing encounters with local men during my visit.

I endured him only because I knew rescue was on its way. Jen—who our friend in common, Amaury Nolasco, had described as, "Swedish, blond and fun, just like you!"—was due in the near future and would be my date for G. Love's show that night. My white rabbit soon pulled up in a Smart Car, gave the Frenchie a definitive "she's coming with me" look, and we scooted away.

From that moment on, Jen became my trusted guide, always appearing when she was most needed. Jen was direct and audacious, yet sweet and shy—a dichotomous personality like the rabbit—and I adored her from the start. We made a quick stop at her apartment just up the street from the café to drop the luggage (me) and make a quick outfit change (her). Then we jumped back in the car and sped off, anxious to get to the concert.

Jen said she was glad for the chance to get away from her usual scene. She managed the bar Lido, a famous old spot with live shows that we'd visit before I left. Hair back in a ponytail, lipstick and mascara applied on the drive—she was also my kind of friend, low maintenance and focused on the fun.

She was less focused on the traffic signs. They're more of a suggestion in Paris anyway. We screeched around a large roundabout and I grabbed the side of the door. It was rare for me to be a passenger but I loved the exhilarating ride—I was usually the crazed driver. The car twisted and turned in what felt like zigzag circles while Jen chattered about the city, half tour guide, half driver. It was perfect, because I was speechless. With the scenery moving by so quickly, I was starting to feel a little like Alice again, and seeing everything through rose-tinted glasses, on top of it. That first day in Paris, moving through the glamorous streets of my childhood dreams, I was definitely in a land of wonder.

Every corner we turned, all I could think was, "When are we going to see the real Paris? This is larger than life, it seems surreal." From the Eiffel Tower to the Place de l'Etoile and through the Arc de Triomphe, I could barely keep up as the miles of cobblestone streets flew by. The last time I remembered feeling this kind of vertigo was my first time in Los Angeles—but by nightfall the Hollywood sign and Sunset Boulevard already felt gorgeous and familiar instead of alien and frightening. I kept that in mind as we careened onward.

As night fell, the surrounding landscape twinkled with lights from the boats and bridges along the Seine River. The moon was full as we arrived at the concert hall for G. Love's show.

Outside, a group of guys was leering and speaking French in a way that made me uncomfortable despite the fact that I had no clue what their words meant. Jen turned and said, "*Allez-vous faire foutre. Laissez-nous tranquilles.*"

They spat right back at her and we continued on inside. She laughed, turned to me, and smiled mischievously when she saw my questioning eyes. "I told them to go to hell," she said.

We laughed, bonding over the cocky Parisian men, and turned our attention to the concert. It was a huge venue, and the "oh-my-god-this-is-Paris" feeling faded just a little. We could almost have been anywhere. There were people of all different ages, sizes, and types. A lot of grungy alternative, teenage girls, and older men—not unlike the mix I might see at the Staples Center in LA.

Grabbing our VIP passes and rushing in, we heard G. Love's "Gimme Some Lovin'," and wanted to be in the middle of it all right away. As we sat down into our seats listening to G, I exhaled deeply. I had heard Garrett, a.k.a. G, perform in Los Angeles on multiple occasions. It still floors me that this skinny white guy can sound like a black man sufferin' through the '20s down South. I can't recall how we met, but it was a long time ago—I think it might have been at a bar one night when I walked right up and invited him to a party. (I've always loved an excuse to talk to people anywhere—gas station, bar, the gym.) Over the years, Garrett has never lost his sense of gratitude toward his fans and friends. He always comes through with tickets and was always ready to take on one of my Angie Big Ideas, like, "Hey Garrett, I know you are busy performing and being a musician but want to come play Nintendo's new Wii Music game at Austin City Limits? You would be great with all the different instruments!" And he came and he was.

It's always fun to have the backstage pass and see the "behind the scenes," but for me what really made the night was having the warm feeling of an old friend and familiar tunes. As I was singing along, I looked around and realized everyone else was too—in English. It made me smile and for that moment, I was at home.

Later that night, as we passed the Eiffel Tower again, I remembered I wasn't—and that was even better.

TRIPPING POINT

Landing in the world's most iconic travel destinations can feel pretty trippy. For the cure, find music,

BIO ▶▶

AMAURY NOLASCO

Amaury Nolasco played the prison innate Fernando Sucre on the TV show "Prison Break." He's from Puerto Rico, where he was studying biology when a casting agent found him and recruited him for his first commercial shoot. I trust Amaury like I trust a brother. He looks the part of scary older protective guy. With his piercing eyes, bald head, and dark muscular physique, you'd think he could squash you like a cream puff—until he smiles and his cheeks become the cream puffs. He only plays the villain in movies.

CHAPTER 12 DONALD SUTHERLAND'S CHICKENS

DESTINATION Bon Marché, Paris

INSPIRATION Donald Sutherland, my favorite old man, inspires me to visit the Bon Marché.

• • • • • • • • • • • • • • • • • • • •

To this day, I am still unsure who told Donald Sutherland to contact me with BlackBerry questions, but I would love to know so I could kiss them. From the day of that blind call from him in 2007, Donald became my oldest role model. He's my "chicken soup for the soul." The first call about BlackBerry turned into so many questions that eventually I had my assistant get his email address. Lucky for me it kicked off, over a span of years, a series of emails that could make me forget daily dramas and suffocating stress. Always entertaining, chock-full of facts and wisdom that only come with age, Donald sends me articles about BlackBerry, stories about meeting political figures, intellectual quotes he enjoys, and tales from his time on set around the world, always signing off in a way that puts a smile on my face.

Donald once used his computer pen to draw a picture of me wearing a white wig. Along with it was a note that went something like this: "Dear, this is you with a white wig just as I imagined before seeing how young you were at your delightful event. I never go to those you know, but I really enjoyed myself."

You might wonder after reading Donald's long email why the story you're getting is the one about chickens. Out of all the fabulous Parisian destinations, why would I choose to go grocery shopping and look at the price of the chickens? Did I mention I'm also a vegetarian?

I loved picturing Donald in France, grocery shopping at the Bon

Angie,

Paris. You'll love it. They have such a fantastic life, the French. Theirs is what Paul Krugman in his column in the NYTimes called the true 'family values'. Health care, wonderful education, long family vacations, no shopping on Sunday so the people stay at home for a lunch with all the generations around the table. The food is extraordinary. Even the ordinary is extraordinary. If you can, go into the markets, the local one I knew best was in Passy, have a look and you'll get an idea how you eat at home. And you do your shopping every day, for the day, not for the week. Look at the price range of chickens. The really expensive ones are really, really good. Huge difference. The Bon Marché in St. Germain de Prés is a good place to go look at food. At bread and cheese and wine and all the other delicious things they eat at home in France. And they have great clothes and stuff. And go to Rue des Saint Peres because that's where all the shoes are. That's just off Boulevard St Germain. You can have coffee at the Flores, maybe lunch across the street at Lipp. Deux Maggot is there. There's the Parfumier in the Palais Royale, Serge Lutens. I was there a while ago. Mostly I was outside in the park on a bloody conference call with the dog and my wife was in there. The fragrances are only sold in Paris and it's fantastic. Go smell it. I was walking the dog and on a conference call. I was not on a conference call with a dog. You should get a telephone card from the tabac. It used to cost you twenty five dollars and you could call forever, actually three hundred minutes, to pretty much wherever. For a special occasion with friends coming from the States you can take them to eat at Ami Louis. The lamb was wonderful and it's a big favourite of North Americans. The number used to be 0148877748 but that's probably out of date. It's at 32 rue de Vertbois in the 3rd. Stresa is good. Used to be, anyway. Expensive. Italian. Near the Champs Elysees. 7 rue

Chambiges behind the Plaza Athene. Everything is 'used to be' because I haven't been back in a while. Cesar, the sculptor was always there.But he's gone now, of course. Chez Allard on Rue St Andre des Arts near Place St Michel was terrific. An old favourite. So was Chez Josephine on rue du Cherche Midi, (it has another name, but your hotel will know it), and Angelina on rue de Rivoli. It's probably the Frenchest place of the lot. And it's pretty near Faubourg St Honore where Hermes is and that's nice to wander around. Lanvin and the hats at Gelot. Go sit in the Louvre, the Orangerie at the Concorde at the top of the Tuilieries has the water lilies of Monet. The Jeu de Paume which is right beside l'Orangerie and it has modern work. It used to hold impressionists but they moved over to the Gallerie d'Orsay, which used to be the old railway station, when it started up as a gallery in the eighties. The d'Orsay has hanging there the scandalous 'Origin of the World' by Gustave Courbet. It was hidden behind a curtain for years and years. Then Andre Masson painted a painting to cover it so that the collector who owned it could hang it with Masson's picture in front and then take off the Masson when he wanted to show the Courbet. Jim Morrison's buried in the Pere Lachaise Cemetery in Boulevard de Ménilmontant in the 20th if you want to go there. I never saw his grave but the cemetery's fabulous if you like dead people. If you get sick go into a hospital. It's the best health care in the world. Ride the Metro or take a bus. And walk. Repetto on rue Royale sells really comfortable dancer's shoes. Get a map and make sure the GPS on your phone works over there. Haussmann's city is in circles and triangles not rectangles and wandering can get you lost in a second. Which is great, but you need to know how to get back. I'll send this to Rossif and see if he can update it with things that would apply to someone young. You could take a boat ride on the Bateau Mouche at night. And go up to the top of the Eiffel Tower and the Arc de Triomphe. Go into Notre Dame and have ice cream over there. Berthillon. The Ile Saint Louis. Very famous that ice cream. And if you're there on a weekend it's good to go to the Marché Puces. The best part of it was the

Serpette. How long are you there? Where are you staying? Will you need a hairdresser? Have a wonderful trip.

Donald

BIO▼

DONALD SUTHERLAND

Donald Sutherland has most recently appeared as President Snow in "The Hunger Games," but he's been one of Hollywood's most iconic actors since 1970, when he starred as Hawkeye Pierce in Robert Altman's "MASH." The '70s was arguably America's best decade for cinema, and Sutherland acted in some of its best, and strangest gems: "Klute," with Jane Fonda, "Don't Look Now," with Julie Christie, and "Day of the Locust." He's been making interesting, acclaimed films ever since, and in 2011, got his star on the Hollywood Walk of Fame.

CHICKENS IN PARIS

"CHICKENS IN PARIS ARE THE BEST IN THE WORLD. NOT BE-CAUSE THEY'RE WELL COOKED: THEY'RE NOT. BUT BECAUSE OF THE QUALITY OF FRENCH CHICK-EN, AND THE FACT THAT ONLY FRENCH PEOPLE (AND ONLY A SMALL NUMBER OF THEM) ARE READY TO PAY THE PRICE THAT A GOOD QUALITY CHICKEN COSTS. THAT'S BECAUSE REALLY GOOD CHICKEN (GAULOISE BLANCHE, BRESSE, GÉLINE DE TOURAINE) REQUIRES A LONG GROWTH–UP TO 120 DAYS FOR SOME OF THEM, AS OPPOSED TO LESS THAN 40 FOR THE CRAPPIEST CHICKEN–AND A LOT OF FREE SPACE EACH, UP TO A FEW SQUARE METERS PER CHICKEN, AS OPPOSED TO 20 CHICKEN PER SQUARE METER FOR SAID CRAPPIEST. THAT RE-SULTS IN VERY HIGH INDIVIDUAL COSTS–EASILY 16€/KG (THAT'S $9/LB), SO THAT A REALLY NICE CHICKEN CAN COST NORTH OF 30€. –FROM CHOWHOUND.COM

Marché. I wanted to step into his wise old-man shoes and follow their steps. Who thinks, when they go on vacation, "I must get to the grocery store to truly explore?" When someone else describes the moment, it adds an element of adventure, especially knowing you are going to report back.

Finally, I was ready to do something normal. Traveling, you start miss the routines from home, like grocery shopping. A simple task with a fascinating twist, when abroad: all the different kinds of chips, candy flavors, and exotic foods. It's fun to see what foreigners come up with— their brand names, packaging (Dijon mustard in juice glasses, covered in kids' cartoons!), and random flavors.

Paris' Bon Marché is a dream. Everything seems fresh and exciting and new. I swear I went through every aisle at least twice and watched others shop, too. Everything seemed so different, from the dusty wooden floors to the cheese mongers, who seemed to so thoroughly enjoy their time helping shoppers find just the right cheese for their feast.

Don't get me wrong: I'm sure my Whole Foods has a guy who experiences similar rapture while talking about cheese. But at home I am blinded by my BlackBerry and on autopilot with thoughts of my night plans or the boy I want to call me. Here, I soaked up the moment. Away from my usual day-to-day, living someone else's day-to-day from 30 years ago in a place unlike any I'd ever seen.

I found the chickens and was amazed to see what Donald was talking about: Prices went up to about $40 at the high end, for a tiny little chicken. I got proof with a photo from the handy BlackBerry, taken by the first passerby I could grab, an Asian women who crinkled her brow but snapped the picture anyway. Then we both got in trouble, when an employee appeared and informed me that there was no photography allowed in the store. In Paris, shops are for shopping. Voila.

I emailed Donald the pictures and his email back made me happier than the grocery adventure itself. Like me, he likes side tangents, but always finishes in a way that makes you feel like you really know him. His emails are usually stories that teach me lessons. Sharing moments can be even more satisfying than living them.

TRIPPING POINT

There's unique joy in helping someone reconnect with a memory. Even if the memory is of a chicken.

CHAPTER 13 PUTTIN' ON THE RITZ

DESTINATION Hemingway Bar at the Ritz Carlton, Paris
INSPIRATION Will Kopelman suggests that I order a drink
from the world's greatest bartender.

• • • • • • • • • • • • • • • • • • •

The Ritz Carlton in Paris is dauntingly grand and historic, but the
Hemingway Bar in the back is a living room. It's small enough to feel
intimate but large enough to be able to have a private moment at your
own table. I knew from the little I'd read that the bar is patronized by an
international smattering of diplomats, bankers, fashion models, play-
boys, and tycoons. Kevin Nealon had written me that it was the place
where Diana had been last before the crash that took her life.

Paris was Hemingway's inspiration—Paris with its food and drink.
Mostly drink. Seems that every two pages Hemingway was downing a
brandy, a beer, or a whiskey. In any case, this bar got its name because
the writer famously ordered a drink here during the liberation of Paris
while gunfire from retreating Nazi soldiers could still be heard outside.
Apparently, not even war or the threat of speeding bullets could distract Hemingway from his pursuit of booze.

As I settled in, I opened my pink journal and flipped to Will Kopelman's email, recommending that I visit the Hemmingway haunt to find a
bartender named Colin.

Looking up at the bar, I knew the man behind it had to be Colin. He
upheld the grandeur of the Ritz, standing elegantly behind the bar with his
wire rim glasses and white blazer, and a Mona Lisa smile. I felt the familiar
excited anticipation that comes with meeting someone new, and knowing I would hear a new success story to remind me what we can do

Thanks for this!

I found the part about Rao's funny because though I totally agree (Frankie's been like a second uncle to me growing up, and one of my dad's fondest friends), as we both know, not anybody can just walk into Rao's because they heard it was a great place to visit! That aside, here's my two cents:

Paris: go to the Hemingway bar in the back of the Ritz hotel. It's a tiny bar on the Rue Cambon side of the hotel where Ernest Hemingway used to hang out when he lived in Paris. The bartender, Colin should still be there. He's a fixture of the joint. Tell him you're friends with the Kopelmans, and have him surprise you with his best seasonal drink. He's a master. One of the best small little bars in France; and when I say small I mean tiny.

with drive and motivation.

To be honest, I was nervous. Yes, I was meeting a bartender—but in the bar of the Paris Ritz. One who I had read about in *Forbes*, celebrated as the world's greatest bartender.

I leaned in, trying to be coy, but then burst out with a rush of words.

"Colin—are you *the* Colin of the Hemingway Bar? My friend Will Kopelman has sent me to meet you!"

Colin laughed, "Ah yes! The Kopelmans! Such a lovely family and Will has spent quite a few fun nights here at the Hemingway Bar."

Colin quickly got down to the business of taking my order. I asked him to surprise me, as Will had suggested. Then I watched him go to work, disappearing to the back to gather supplies. He returned carrying a martini glass of yellow dandelion-colored drink, with half of a passion fruit floating in its center. Colin explained that I was to use the straw to suck out the strawberry-infused vodka and then remove the half passion fruit and drink up.

It was sweet and strong—and unbelievably delicious.

I asked Colin about his work at the Ritz and he described his entrepreneurial vision for bartenders and mixologists. He had taught courses and created training programs for bartenders around the world. His philosophy is that bartending is about so much more than making drinks. It is about people and culture and understanding the world. This was before anyone really knew about mixology, and Colin had been practicing it for years! I felt adrenaline kick in just hearing his visionary approach first hand.

Colin's work has brought him into contact with incredible people. Charles Veley, who he had just met that week, was a story that seemed to be created just for me! Charles is the world's most traveled person. At age 37 he became the youngest recorded person to visit all the countries of the world as defined by the Traveler's Century Club. He created a "Master List" that currently has 872 countries. No one has visited them all, but Veley has come closest, at 822.

I left the Ritz that day feeling that I had met an artist—not just with alcohol but in helping others live. Colin is the type of man you want to be, to know, or at the very least be around. Colin makes you think without knowing you are thinking. He makes you feel at ease without even realizing you were uncomfortable. I found myself wanting to write down every word that he spoke, but decided to sit and listen instead.

Will completely understood my search for inspiration when he gave me Colin. Leaving him, I felt inspired to make my own story worth someday being retold by the world's greatest bartender.

I had some work to do.

WORLD'S GREATEST BARTENDER

"OVER THE PAST 18 YEARS, COLIN FIELD HAS MADE THE HEMING-
WAY BAR OF THE RITZ PARIS THE CITY'S PRE-EMINENT WATERING
HOLE. MORE THAN A BARTENDER, MR. FIELD IS A HOST WITH A
KNACK FOR SPARKING CONVERSATION BETWEEN HIS GUESTS
AND APPROACHES DRINK-MAKING WITH THE DETAILED EYE OF
A TAILOR, OFTEN SIZING UP A CUSTOMER'S PERSONALITY AND
MOOD TO CREATE A MADE-TO-MEASURE COCKTAIL. CONSIDERED
BY MANY TO BE ONE OF PARIS'S BEST BARTENDERS, HE WILL
SOON BECOME THE TOWN'S MOST SOUGHT-AFTER ONE AS THE
RITZ PREPARES TO SHUT DOWN FOR A TWO-YEAR RENOVATION
ON APRIL 16." –FROM *THE WALL STREET JOURNAL*

"IF YOU ARE GOING TO MAKE A COCKTAIL, YOU MUST UNDER-
STAND THE MAN WHO MADE THE ALCOHOL. THE AVERAGE
PERSON MEASURES THE QUALITY OF ALCOHOL ACCORDING TO
THE PRICE, WHICH IS NOT NECESSARILY RIGHT; YOU NEED TO
KNOW WHO MADE IT AND WHY. TAKE A MASTER BLENDER SUCH
AS RICHARD PATTERSON [OF WHYTE AND MACKAY], WHO MAKES
FABULOUS WHISKIES ON JURA. HE IS AN ARTIST AND IS TRY-
ING TO SAY THINGS WITH HIS ALCOHOL, TRYING TO CREATE AN
INHERENT QUALITY OF THE ISLAND AND BALANCE BETWEEN BIT-
TERNESS AND SWEETNESS. THEN YOU GET PEOPLE WHO WORK
BEHIND A BAR FOR THE SUMMER AND CALL THEMSELVES A BAR-
TENDER, AND THEY GRAB THIS BOTTLE HE HAS BEEN WORKING
ON FOR 20 YEARS (HE'S DEVOTED HIS LIFE TO IT, LIKE MASTER
DISTILLER WILLIE TAIT) AND THEY RIP OFF THE TOP AND MIX IT
WITH PINEAPPLE JUICE AND GRENADINE. FOR ME, IT IS A RELAY
RACE. I GRAB THAT BATON FROM RICHARD AND HAVE TO WIN THE
RACE FOR HIM. IT'S ABOUT RESPECT OF THE EARTH, THE DIS-
TILLER, THE PRODUCTS, THE ALEMBICS, THE THICKNESS OF THE
COPPER, THE WAY IT WAS HEATED, EVERYTHING, OTHERWISE
YOU CAN'T MAKE A COCKTAIL." –COLIN FIELDS, IN AN INTERVIEW
FOR *THE CONNEXTION*

FROM **Kevin Nealon**
TO **Angie Banicki**
subject **30 before 30**

Susan and I went to Paris last year. At the time we were reading the Princess Diana book since it was, I think the 10th anniversary of her death and the book was relatively new and good.

We visited (actually stayed at the Ritz Hotel) and pretty much retraced her footsteps from the Hemingway Bar in the hotel to the nearby tunnel where their car crashed. We even rode up in the same elevator in the hotel. Sort of morbid but also nostalgic.

I think there's also a famous tower in Paris you may want to check out.

Have a great trip and maybe we'll see you on Wed. at the book signing.

Kevin

TRIPPING POINT

No matter how well traveled you become, there will always be someone who's done more.

BIO ▶▶

WILL KOPELMAN

Will's email responding to my 30 Before 30 request was special because travel connected us. I knew Will as a staple on our H&S party guest lists, and I was excited to get a glimpse into his real life and learn that he wanted to share in my adventure. Will, an art advisor and curator known for his taste and intelligence, is now married to Drew Barrymore. When I met Drew, before she was with Will, I told her about my 30 before 30 too (or actually Harley Pasternak told her about it—yes it was at the gym). She responded as enthusiastically as Will, saying she wanted to travel with inspiration, too. A perfect match—one I wish I could take the credit for setting up.

CHAPTER 14 SHAMELESS SHOPPING

DESTINATION Vintage Shopping, Paris
INSPIRATION Emmy Rossum decodes Paris' vintage scene.

• • • • • • • • • • • • • • • • • • • •

People say they go to Paris or Rome and are inspired to dress just a little bit better. Emmy Rossum inspired me to try.

I am no fashionista. In fact, I've been known to wear workout clothes to certain occasions of the non-exercise kind—and without knowing if it is appropriate or not. PS, I was once hired for a job in my running shorts.

Jessica Paster, a celebrity stylist who's actually dressed Emmy Rossum as well, has scolded me multiple times for wearing tennis shoes with skirts, having stains on my dresses, and mismatching accessories with clothing.

She once wrote on my FB wall, "Angie, you are a beautiful girl with gorgeous legs but you've got to stop dressing like you are going to the barn to feed the animals."

And so, as I walked the streets of Paris armed with Emmy's incredible guide to all the great vintage shops, I was impressed but not really buying. Shopping is not as much fun alone—and I needed those credit cards to pay for experiences. Window shopping and chatting with the chic store clerks gave me all I needed from fashion in Paris.

That said, I had to include Emmy's recommendations here. They're too good for all the true fashionistas to miss!

FIRST of all, THANK YOU for including me in this email chain! Its an
honor that you think of me like that! and CONGRATS, you are going
to have a wonderful time!

PARIS!

only my favorite city in the whole world! obviously go to eiffel
tower. its really stunning at sunset! and it normally is all lit up with
sparkly lights at night

you MUST go to LA DUREE bakery/restaurant on the champs elysee
and eat the MACAROONS. take some home with you. they last about
a week and are the MOST DELICIOUS THING IN THE WORLD (they
are also actually sold in london in harrods food court by the candy
section but somehow taste much better in paris!)

SHOP! heres a list of great shopping!

-Mona, Rue Bonaparte, 6th -fun mix of designer clothes and accessories (mcqueen,lanvin, pierre hardy)

-Montaigne Market, Avenue Montaigne, 8th -great designer stuff
(lanvin,alaia,givenchy)

Iris, Rue de Grenelle, 7th - amazing shoes

-Sabia Rosa, 7th - beautiful lingerie

-L'Eclarier, 4th - more great designer (balenciaga, chloe, rick owens)
New Rick Owens and Marc Jacobs stores in the Palais Royal

-Didier Ludot, Palais Royal 2nd - incredible vintage, but insanely
overpriced Gabrielle Geppert, Palais Royal, 2nd - cute vintage
finds, great accessories

-Iglaine, 2nd - random selection of vintage, but some rare vintage
Alaias that are incredibly priced

-Quidam de Revel, 4th - appointment only vintage store

The 1st and 8th have the best designer stores. The Marais and St. Germain des Pres are ideal for small boutiques and vintage

MOST OF ALL! HAVE FUN! BREATHE IN THE AIR! REMEMBER THAT EVERY MEMORY YOU MAKE YOU WILL HAVE FOREVER! KEEP A JOURNAL OF FUNNY THING AND MAKE SURE TO TAKE A TON OF PICTURES!!!!!!!!!

i am so happy for you!

love
emmy

BIO▶▶

EMMY ROSSUM

Emmy Rossum is not just an actress with a beautiful voice, though she is that. She's played the leads in films like "Phantom of the Opera" and "Songcatcher," and now is the star of "Shameless," opposite William H. Macy. Emmy is actually a smart young entrepreneur and this is what drew me in the first time I met her. I've enjoyed watching her stardom rise in tandem with her business acumen as she markets her first album. On top of all that, she somehow knows how to make a farmer's outfit look like fashion. Perhaps it runs in the family—Vera Wang is her aunt!

MONA

OWNER MONA BLONDE COMMISSIONED PHILIPPE STARCK'S FORMER ASSISTANT, CHRISTIAN GAVOILLE, TO DESIGN A CONTEMPORARY INTERIOR WITH TRADITIONAL INFLUENCES. THE RESULT IS A FAUX FASHION SHOW SETTING—COMPLETE WITH EDITOR SEATS—HEAVILY ACCENTED WITH ROUGE AND PORCELAIN COLORS FROM CARAVAGGIO'S PAINTINGS. OF COURSE, NO SHOW WOULD BE COMPLETE WITHOUT MODEL, DROOL-WORTHY DESIGNER DUDS, "IT" BAGS, AND KILLER STILETTOS FROM LANVIN, AZZEDINE ALAÏA, STELLA MCCARTNEY, AND ALEXANDER MCQUEEN, AND SHOES BY BOTTEGA VENETTA AND PIERRE HARDY.

TRIPPING POINT

Paris is to fashion as animal is to farm. You don't have do farms or fashion to have a good time grazing in both.

CHAPTER 15 NE-YO, LADY V, ST. T AND ME

DESTINATION Villa Romana Hotel, Nikki Beach, and a couple of big yachts in St. Tropez

INSPIRATION Lady Victoria Hervey invites me to a party in St. Tropez with co-host Ne-Yo.

● ● ● ● ● ● ● ● ● ● ● ● ● ● ● ● ● ● ●

It was never in the plans to bask in the luxurious St. Tropez in the south of France. The destination felt like it belonged on "Lifestyles of the Rich and Famous," not my inspirational adventure. But Lady Victoria, a well-known model and socialite who I'd heard of but never met, had invited me down for a big party and was making it very hard to say no. It was a nice change to have someone working to get me to a party instead of the other way around.

Tuesday: "Sunday is gonna be big, first the Nikki Beach party then the VIP club that night with DJ mars and Ne-Yo performing…"

Fifty percent, I told Lady V.

Wednesday: "We have a room for you at the hotel. We'll drink rosé and go to fun dinners."

Okay, 75 percent. I was starting to feel overwhelmed by Paris and all the moments I needed to complete.

Thursday: "What percentage, Angie?"

Eighty percent. It was like travel roulette.

Friday: "We have a driver fulltime that can pick u up called François let me know what time your flight arrives!"

OK, I think I'm coming.

I finally committed to giving the luxe life a go.

Did I say the luxe life? When I landed in Toulon, no one exactly rolled out the red carpet. Lady Victoria didn't answer her phone, and so

I tried and tried and waited and waited. Was this the right move? I'm not going to lie, the French scare me. I think part of it is how they spit their words—blunt, unabashed rhetoric with intimidation unrelated to what they're even saying. I mustered up the courage to finally call the hotel. They eventually sent a driver, but not before forcing me to decipher a lot of incomprehensible hacking French.

My driver arrived and grabbed one suitcase with a snap of attitude. His eyes squinted at my airport attire (always exercise clothes, remember?) as I followed him to the car while he hissed at me in dragon-like French. On the drive home, the dragon unleashed himself, zig-zagging over the road. I pretended to be a princess as I slid back and forth in the minivan, grabbing the seat, handlebars, armrests—anything to hold me down and back from flying through the windshield. All I could do was pull out my video camcorder, half-whispering into it with nervous excitement, filming the beautiful rolling hills and luscious green landscape out the window as we whizzed past.

When we finally arrived, and my disheveled self stepped up to the reception desk, the miniature tanned 40ish lady at the front desk looked at me with eyes that said: "And really, what do you think you are doing here?"

"Can I help you?" she said primly.

I stuttered just to get out in English, "Um. I guess. Well. Victoria, who I'm meeting, is probably sleeping…can I just go lie by the pool?"

"Do whatever. You speak no French, do you not? Ugh."

Did she actually say "ugh"?? Her eyes rolled as she spoke French to the two men at the counter, and looked back at me, laughing.

Mortified, I turned and headed to the pool.

There amidst the sparkling blue water, surrounded by chic white cushions, lounges, tables, and curtains, I took a deep breath under the beating sun. The ocean was close enough to see and smell it. One of the very attractive gentlemen attendants who'd witnessed my entry approached as I settled into a white lounge chair—ungracefully—with my dirty travel bag by my side. He smiled and asked if I would care for fruit. Hello glistening bronzed chest, are these grapes for *moi*?

I smiled back prettily—then the lounge tipped to the side and I toppled over, laughing far too loudly to pass as a giggle. I climbed back on and tried to look back up at him with a smile, but he'd already turned to go. I'd barely settled back in when a gorgeous tall blond in purple chiffon and big Dior sunglasses came running over and grabbed me in a big hug.

"Angie, I'm so sorry I wasn't awake when you got in. But you made it! Are you okay? My phone died. We were out late." Yes, this was Victoria. The beautiful woman I'd never met was happy I was here! I felt a sigh of relief escape me. It looked like things were going to start getting easier.

First thing on our agenda was a boat ride—and by boat I mean huge yacht. It wasn't long before we were heading down the beach to the water. As soon as my bare feet touched the warm sand, my worries turned to small crystal grains on the beach, kicked around and buried under the sun. Lady V and I brushed through the glistening sunbathers out to the spot where a dinghy awaited us. The entire time in my head I was the girl walking on the sandy beach pictured in magazines: no thoughts but to take in the beauty surrounding me. We waded out in the cool blue water, climbed into our dinghy, and zoomed off to the yacht.

That dingy pulled me out of the magazine and into a rap video. I've always wanted to shake my booty on a yacht in the water to some Jay Z or T-Pain. Two blondes, shades on, wind in our hair, holding onto that dingy, we wave-zoomed over to the big yacht with an R&B singer rolling up right after us. I felt my booty rearing to shake. We were greeted by a group of pasty white Speedo-clad gay boys. The men had already started the fun and welcomed us, pouring rosé and turning up the south of France Eurod dance tunes.

Ne-Yo, in his preppy attire, Tishawn, and his security man, Carter, and with his security man, Carter, arrived shortly after us, completing

BIO▼

Ne-Yo

When I met Ne-Yo, a.k.a. Shaffer Chimere Smith, he was promoting his third album, "Year of the Gentleman." I love what he told the UK R&B writer Pete Lewis about the thinking behind the title: "To me 'Year Of The Gentleman' is all about a persona, a swag, and a charm. I made an assessment of the music business. And, in my personal opinion, the essence of the gentleman is absent right now. Everybody kinda looks the same, everybody's kinda doing the same thing, everybody's kinda rude and full of themselves. Whereas a gentleman is calm, courteous, kind, charming... So that title basically represents me trying to lead by example, and showing these cats what it is to be a gentleman in this business still." Ne-Yo was exactly those things during the time we spent together—and if you can be a gentleman in St. Tropez, you can be a gentleman anywhere.

ST. TROPEZ

JUST AS GIDGET CHANGED MALIBU FOREVER, FRENCH '50S BOMBSHELL BRIGITTE BARDOT TRANSFORMED THIS ONCE-QUIET BEACH TOWN INTO A MAGNET FOR SOCIAL-ITES AND PLEASURE SEEK-ERS WITH HER MOVIE "AND GOD CREATED WOMAN." THAT REPUTATION CONTINUES TO-DAY. ST. TROPEZ IS KNOWN FOR ITS BEAUTIFUL COTE D'AZUR BEACHES, BOHEMIAN FLAIR AND AN "ANYTHING GOES" SPIRIT THAT HAD STARLETS PIONEERING NUDE BEACHES HERE AS EARLY AS THE 1930S.

quite the scene.

I watched as Victoria nervously reconfirmed details for the party that Ne-Yo was hosting and rattled off other offers she'd received for him, all while making sure everyone was having a good time. It was fascinating to watch her do "my job"—and nice to see that Angie Panicki syndrome wasn't limited to me. My only job for now was to bask in the fact that I had no plans to adhere to and to enjoy whatever St. Tropez gave me. I sat back and soaked in the sun with my rosé and pondered the difference between a vacationer and an adventurer. I was definitely the latter, but even an adventurer needs a vacation. Right?

Under the influence of the sun and two or maybe three rosés, I fell asleep on a large white seat surrounded by pillows, only to wake up later to see that a photo shoot of me had gone on while I was passed out. It seems an impression had been made—I had now gone from quiet girl to lightweight.

"You were so adorable. An early siesta, Miss Banicki!" Victoria said as everyone laughed.

I jumped right up, ready to go again after my rest. We danced it up, "I'm on a boat" style (as one can only do on an actual boat) before heading back to the hotel for a rest and outfit change.

Dinnertime schedules in the south of France go something like this:

10:00 p.m.–Siesta–I obviously had mine a little early that day, so I caught up on work while the others napped.
11:00 p.m.–Dress and prepare to go out for dinner.
12:00 a.m.–Dinner, our reservation for Villa Romana.

In the 11 p.m. period, I tried to find a dress appropriate for St. Tropez style. Every time I held up a dress or tried one on, then turned to Victoria, she'd say, "No, nope, let's see what else you've got."

Finally, when I put on my go-to black dress, she said, "I have it. Wear this Missoni, I'm not wearing it and it'll look gorgeous on you."

How could I say no? I felt like Cinderella as I put on the jeweled

117

vintage dress.

By midnight I was starving and we were behind schedule but at 12:15 a.m,. as we stepped into the circus of St. Tropez at the Villa Romana, my hunger was gone as my eyes took in the sights. From animal costumes to firing sparklers, my senses overloaded like I was a kid walking into a circus ring. Gorillas yelling, naked girls strutting, waiters dancing, and punch bowls toppling. Miniature tubs of cocktails overwhelmed the tables with bright obnoxious straws stretching three feet long, jutting out and taunting guests to sip their mysterious potion.

When I said circus, did I mention the clowns? By that I mean the red-lipped, big-eyed, jewelry laden, busty busts of every wealthy woman who swiveled her hips through the door. Each was more outrageous than the last. With bosoms perkier than mine and faces made up like showgirls, I couldn't help but stare.

To complement the clowns, there was eye candy for the gentlemen: bare-breasted models walking the aisles. I was all eyes, and here the normal rules of dinner need not apply; turning in my seat and pointing was welcomed. Half of the clowns (yes, I mean the 60-year-old women) had jumped up onto the tables and were dancing mid-meal. It was no rules and no expense spared. Blame it on the boogie? I probably would have been appalled in L.A. but here I let my dancing queen out and hopped up with them.

Reminder—it was midnight and the night had just begun. I had no items to cross off my list, only to live in that moment with new friends. With Lady V as my tour guide, all I had to do was sit back and relax. She was me, and I was someone else. This weekend, I didn't need to be Promoter Angie, Taskmaster Angie, or even Adventurer Angie. I could relax and be Vacationer Angie. For the moment, that felt like just the right idea.

This was vacation for the rich and famous. I was neither, and living like I was both—for forty-eight hours. Forty-eight hours away from the challenges, the planning, and expectations. Even as I thought it, I felt guilty. Should I be writing? Volunteering? Doing something to help others?

Not tonight. I'd enjoy it, and find a way to pay it forward.

▰ TRIPPING POINT ▰

Sometimes it's OK to let someone else do the work when you travel—your only job is to be dancing on the table at the end of the night.

CHAPTER 16 DAISIES AND DUKES IN VERSAILLES

DESTINATION Versailles and Père-Lachaise Cemetery, Paris

INSPIRATION Jessica and Ashlee Simpson send me to two unusual "romantic" spots.

• • • • • • • • • • • • • • • • • • • •

Everyone wants a love story from Paris.

Unfortunately, I learned pretty quickly that Paris didn't want to give one to me.

The men there are extreme: They either love you or they hate you. First there was the hating cabbie who yelled at me, took more money, then dropped me off six blocks early and practically spat in my face. Next, the waiter who told me, "no English," but then when frustrated, yelled at me in perfect English. Then there was the guy in the park with his hands down his pants, staring and grunting as I ran past him. And finally Julian, my full-blown stalker, who—within 10 minutes of harassing me at a café—decided I was brilliant, beautiful, and an inspiration to all men, then proceeded to email me seven times a day during my entire trip. And by the way, what makes these men think it's attractive to meow at women? I heard men do this twice in as many days, and had one pretend to paw me. When I straight out asked, "Are you for real? Taking cat calls to the extreme?" he said this was a Frenchman's unique way with women.

Needless to say, I was not in a particularly romantic mood that day. Yet I still decided to visit the spot Jessica Simpson had described as Paris' most romantic—Versailles. I would be balancing it with a trip to the Père-Lachaise cemetery, where Ashlee had gone, a good antidote to any romance-overkill in the gardens. Plus, both seemed like ideal places for some reflection time, away from the men of Paris.

Versailles is about 10 miles southwest of Paris' center, and a serene escape from the city's bustle. But approaching the grounds, my initial experience was overwhelming. Hundreds of people were waiting in front of the huge museum at the Versailles entrance, and I started to wish I had holed up in a coffee shop for the day. Once I had made my way through the crowds, I stood timidly near the huge estate museum, shuffling the pebbles under my feet, wondering what I had been thinking by leaving my cozy Parisian café.

Looking down at the vast expanse, I felt immediate release. Lush endless greens, flowers of every shape and color placed just so, marble figurines dotting the floral landscape. I was comforted by the enormity of it all.

Here in the Queen's courtyard, I did notice many couples holding hands with glistening diamond wedding bands, eyes gushing with love.

And so here it was—love all around me. The etymology of Versailles comes from the Latin word *versare,* meaning, "to keep turning, turn over and over." I ended up doing that as I walked, thinking of love.

Everyone I knew had been convinced that if I didn't come back from my 30 Before 30 engaged, I'd at least come back with 30 new belt notches. It was quickly becoming apparent why travel is so often linked with romance. After two weeks of adventuring in the unknown, my ego was dissipating. Slowly travel was peeling away my high fashion uniform and letting the child underneath peek out—the child we all have in us who loves to play and explore. The more I let the child out, the more attention I received from men. Add in the mystery of traveling solo, and I was a man magnet—whether I was interested or not.

Versare, versare…

Still a child scrambling her way out of her parents' arms to run free, I wasn't ready to settle down. My trip was about embracing that child who had forced herself to be adult in the real world. I decided that whenever I was told I needed to settle down, think about the future, usher in romance, I would bring myself back to this labyrinth. My adventure in the maze of greens before me—the place laden with trees of all unique shapes and sizes, branches reaching out to scratch and hold me, paths begging me to walk with them to hidden new places, and calming greens familiar and established, not going anywhere—was a reminder that nature is its own romance. I would embrace that inner child and remind her she could take her time.

FROM **Jessica Simpson**
TO **Angie Banicki**
subject **Re:**

You have to go to Versailles outside of Paris. Someone very special to me sent me a picture of an older couple lying on the lawn so in love. I have since traveled there and it is one of the most romantic places I have ever been. My sister went to the cemetery in Paris where Jim Morrison was buried, and got lost in there for like 2 hours and never found his gravesite.

BIO⬇

JESSICA SIMPSON

Jessica and I met when she sang "The Star Spangled Banner" at my event for the Elizabeth Glaser Pediatric AIDS Foundation. Today she's a mom and I imagine feels love at depths she couldn't yet imagine back at Versailles. I don't think I could handle the cruelty of the tabloids, but somehow Jessica owns who she is and doesn't seem to let it take her down.

Versare, versare...

My last memory of love was of drowning—when it ended, I cried for an entire year, flooding into two. Too much, my friends said. When love slices you that deeply, you find places hurting that you didn't even know existed. And once you know they are there, you can't imagine opening them up again. But you do.

Versare, versare...

Then there's Grandma Banicki. She was married to my grandfather for 50 years and she knows it was worth it even after the hurt of my grandfather's death. Widowed over a year and looking for love for us both, she reminds me to enjoy the journey. Sort of.

> **PÈRE-LACHAISE CEMETERY**
>
> THE CEMETERY IS ON BOULEVARD DE MÉNILMONTANT AND IS HOME TO 2-3 MILLION DEAD PEOPLE, INCLUDING OSCAR WILDE, CHOPIN, EDITH PIAF, GERTRUDE STEIN, AND JIM MORRISON. AFTER MORRISON'S DEATH IN 1971, HIS GRAVE THERE WAS INITIALLY UNMARKED. WHEN THE CEMETERY DID ADD A STONE AND LATER A BUST, THEY WERE COVERED IN FAN GRAFFITI AND EVENTUALLY STOLEN. TODAY A SIMPLE, FENCED-OFF STONE BEARS THE MESSAGE, IN GREEK, "ACCORDING TO HIS OWN DAIMON."

"Angela, do you have a boyfriend yet? That's okay...you'll find one soon....but you better hurry."

Grandma, how are you feeling today? "I'm a little cold....I need a boyfriend."

"Angela you look pretty—and skinny. Don't get too skinny, though. The guys like a little *dupa* to grab onto. I never had a *dupa*." (A "dupa" is Polish for ass.)

"Your mom loves your father so much. She's the best cook I've ever seen. You better be getting tips from her for your husband. Or that's okay. I can't cook either, just stay pretty."

Grandma brings me back to the comedy of romance, a good place to be.

Versare and Versailles complete, I exited the labyrinth.

With a fresh perspective, I headed toward the cemetery in search of Jim Morrison's grave, which I found in 10 minutes flat. Standing at the grave, humming his tunes, were two hippy lovers mourning his loss and celebrating his life. They seemed so content. They'd completed their journey in search of each other and it had led them here. To this couple, Jim Morrison embodied romance.

I wonder what it will look like, feel like, seem like for me? For now, I'm still on my solo journey. But when I recognize myself sharing in a moment like that with someone, I'll know.

Otherwise Grandma Banicki will take me out.

TRIPPING POINT

Whatever the size of your dupa, traveling makes you a magnet for romance. Whether you invite it in is up to you.

CHAPTER 17 THE WIZARD OF LA PLAGE

DESTINATION La Plage, Paris

INSPIRATION Eva Longoria's advice to eat the ravioli and meet the owner there.

● ● ● ● ● ● ● ● ● ● ● ● ● ● ● ● ● ● ●

The day that I planned to hit La Plage started with a long, dreamy walk, finishing at La Musée d'Orsay, where Cassian Elwes had encouraged me to explore the cinematography exhibit (when I'd seen him in London.)

A woman my mother's age offered to take my photo when she saw me awkwardly posing and clicking, attempting to capture a shot of myself holding an apple with a faraway statue involved. High culture at its best.

I thanked her and, examining me with mother's eyes, she asked why I was by myself. I gave a quick summary of my traveling adventure, including Eva Longoria's dinner suggestion, and then was on my way.

An hour later, still not having found a cinematography section (the best and maybe only way to keep me at a museum that long is to give me something hard to find), I was exploring the photography when the same woman approached with an apologetic smile.

"Thank God I found you! Could you tell me the restaurant where Eva Longoria likes to eat? My husband is dying to know. I told him about your trip and he wants to go to her favorite spot for dinner to-night." Despite her teasing eye roll, I could see how excited she was to gift her husband with this knowledge.

Happy to share one of my moments and thrilled that this surrogate mom now approved of my adventure, I pull out my trusty color-coded journal.

"La Plage. I think it means 'the beach' in French."

She beamed, "Thank you! You made my husband a happy man. You have no idea—he loves Eva Longoria!"

Little did she know their excitement put a smile on my face for the rest of the day. I hadn't given them the name of the owner mentioned by Eva, though. I was saving that for myself.

It was past 9 p.m. when I finally went for my run along the River Seine that summery July evening. It was still light under the most beautiful dark-pink tinted sky as the Eiffel Tower twinkled on, as it did every night at 10 p.m. on the dot. I stopped and stood on the Pont du Change bridge and watched the tower sparkle. Beneath the summer stars, I felt recharged and especially independent. Tonight I decided I would travel solo to meet this famed Toto. I knew my friend Jen and current host in Paris had wanted to join me, but I was relishing this day by myself.

I showered quickly, realizing that I was now so hungry I could eat a small animal—and I don't eat meat. Since it was almost too late for dinner, I didn't bother to call the restaurant for a reservation; I threw on a summer dress and jumped in a cab.

"La Plage! Hungry! …I mean hurry."

I hurried down the Port de Javel Haut, spotted the boat-like restaurant on the water, and ran on board to the door.

Taken aback by the trendy interior of the restaurant, a shored boat with creamy cushion chairs, dark accents, and twinkling lights along the water, I was touched—sad even, immediately regretting my decision to come alone. This was the kind of place I wanted to walk into with a girlfriend or even a date to romanticize about a life abroad. It was the kind of restaurant I lived for—lots of character but trendy and chic. This was no tourist trap. Inside the people were French and fabulous. These, finally, were the Parisians I had been looking for!

FROM   Eva Longoria
TO   Angie Banicki
subject **30 Before 30**

La Plage...the best ravioli. It is dinner on a boat that doesn't move.
Toto is the owner, ask for him!

BIO⬇

EVA LONGORIA

Gorgeous Eva Longoria shares top
billing on a hot, long-running show
with three other women, so you might
expect her to be a diva. She is the opposite: kind, appreciative, and sweet
at every event of mine she ever came
to. My client at BlackBerry had a huge
crush on her, and she was always
lovely and charming in indulging him
with lines like, "Tell Paul I'm using my
BBery on the set of 'Desperate House-
wives'!" On top of being a supporter
and spokesperson for several nonprof-
its, Longoria founded Eva's Heroes, a
charity which helps developmentally
disabled children.

I walked right up to the young hostess.

"Is Toto here? Eva Longoria told me about this place. I'm here to
eat but wanted to say hi. I know I don't have a reservation." I rambled
on and when I came up for air, she looked at me and sighed.

"J'ne sais pas. My English *un peu."*

Crap. Language barriers. I went with a simpler approach:
"Is there a Toto here?"

She put her finger up and walked away.

When she returned, a man walked closely behind with a very confused look on his face. He spoke in broken English.

"Hello. I am RJ. I am one of the owners."

His dark hair, kind eyes, and the way he leaned in slightly to help reminded me of my roommate's boyfriend in L.A., who called himself my "guardian angel." Over the course of my trip, I kept finding myself doing this—putting foreign people and things in old, familiar categories until they created their own space in my new reality.

After spending the past days on high alert around Frenchmen, this friendly, "familiar" face was a welcome change. Completely at ease, I explained my mission.

"Toto?"

He seemed surprised.

"Yes, isn't the owner here? His name is Toto, right?"

"He is, but not tonight. Come back tomorrow."

He must've sensed disappointment in my eyes. "You want a drink?" he asked, motioning to the bar along the wall as though it

LA PLAGE PARISIENNE

"BETWEEN PONT MIRABEAU AND THE SHORES OF THE ÎLE AUX CYGNES IN THE 15TH DISTRICT, THIS SANDLESS BEACH (PLAGE) RESEMBLES THE FAMOUS DEAUVILLE BOARDWALK. HERE YOU CAN ENJOY A FUN AND TRENDY ATMOSPHERE AND REFINED CUISINE BY THE SEINE RIVER WHILE WATCHING THE SEAGULLS FLIT ABOUT AS THEY FOLLOW THE LAZY PASSAGE OF BOATS AND OTHER BATEAUX-MOUCHES. SPECIAL MENTION FOR THE DESSERT TRAY AND CHARMING, EFFICIENT SERVICE!" –FROM BESTRESTAURANTSPARIS.COM would soften the news.

"No. No. I'm staying for dinner. I'm starving. Do you have a spot for me?" I turned back to ask the hostess.

"Alone?" RJ asked. When I nodded, he seemed appalled.

"You don't speak French, no? No matter, you can't sit alone. Come with me."

He felt bad and wanted to take care of me. Was this possible, a Parisian man with kind intentions? Maybe this was my French guardian angel. He was so warm and his eyes said all I needed to know. I shrugged my shoulders and followed.

Dorothy, we're not in Kansas anymore.

He turned as we walked. "Come meet the other owners and architects. They have been drinking wine. I warn you."

We approached a large, low-set table with eight men laughing and drinking wine around it. They pushed finished dinner plates aside and welcomed me in. Between them and across from me sat a gorgeous model who I found out later was an interior designer from Africa and the wife of the handsome Parisian investor sitting to her right. We sat on pillows on the ground around the table overflowing with half-eaten dishes, bottles of wine—rosés, sauvignon blanc—and a mixture of sweets.

I couldn't wipe the grin off my face, realizing how lucky I had been to show up alone. The stars and my own intuition had been right after all. If even one friend had been with me, I would never have been invited into their circle.

"What would you like to eat?" RJ asked.

He couldn't have asked me a more enticing question. I was beyond ravenous.

"I was sent for the ravioli! Do you have that? But I feel bad, you've already eaten?"

"Don't be silly—tonight we try new dishes and ones we like! We

131

don't have the ravioli."

"What do you suggest? I'll eat anything, I'm just hungry!"

Then I remembered that I actually won't eat anything.

"Actually, I don't eat meat...but anything else," I added shyly.

RJ, in shock asked, "No meat?!" The pretty woman winked at me in understanding.

"OK, fish though, yes? I will order you vegetables and sea bass!"

Gulping rosé in anticipation of food, I watched RJ instruct the waiter and then chef to make a special order for me. I now realized that this was Toto's partner. He later introduced me to Jean Pierre, their other partner. RJ, an excellent host, made certain I was comfortable. By the time I'd finished my first glass of rosé, I had been drawn into their stories and laughing as if I'd known them for ages. Where had this Paris been all along?!

An older gentleman had moved his way down the table and kept interrupting the conversation, trying to convince me he was Toto. I humored him as he told his tales.

"He is not Toto. Just ignore him," RJ and the other men told me, rolling their eyes and laughing. "Be good, Sebastian!"

But I enjoyed the side distraction, since the table would sometimes get caught up in conversation and forget they'd switched to French. Nila, the beautiful model across from me, always made sure to explain, but I was comfortable with the flow between the languages. It was enough to be witness to such a loving and happy group. My new guardians had taken me under their wing.

I couldn't stop laughing and teasing Sebastian, the old-man architect who kept assuring me his name was Toto. His harmless flirting was ultimately my favorite part of the night. Eventually, his friend smiled apologetically, taking Sebastian's arm as they escorted him to a cab, but not before Sebastian took my hand, saying, "You and me, we will run away. I, Toto, will take you to tour the countryside with me. You will like?!"

The men at the table were rolling with laughter. The family had sent home their drunk uncle.

As new and old friends joined our table, I saw that I was just one of the new friends welcomed in. RJ and Jean Pierre tried to speak as much English as they could, introducing me to everyone while making fun of me like their new little sister, keeping my wine glass full, and ensuring I ate and enjoyed. I couldn't have asked for a better night.

When the clock struck midnight, I felt I'd overstayed my welcome and I decided to make the journey home so that I would be fresh for the next day. To my surprise, they wouldn't hear of it.

"No. No. Stay. You cannot leave!"

But I said my *au revoirs* and left with smiles and kisses all around. I knew as I stepped through the doors that I'd be back. After all, I had to meet Toto.

TRIPPING POINT

Never eat alone—but sometimes starting solo, with your guard down, is the best way make new friends.

CHAPTER 18 THE KISSING BANDIT STRIKES

DESTINATION Hotel Costes, Paris

INSPIRATION "Grey's Anatomy" star Ellen Pompeo encourages me to check out Hotel Costes in Paris.

• • • • • • • • • • • • • • • • • • • •

"**J**e suis désolé. Je suis désolé. Je suis désolé."

I repeated the phrase, despite the eye roll of my cabbie as he sped toward La Plage for my second night in a row there. I had asked him to teach me "I'm so sorry," in French, to which he had replied matter of factly, "The French do not say, 'I'm sorry.'"

"It doesn't matter. Just tell me." I insisted, although I believed, based on experience, that he was right.

"But in Paris there are no apologies."

"Please!" I pleaded.

New phrase memorized, the cab pulled up and I jumped out, 30 minutes late for my second visit to La Plage. I was prepared to work hard to win over Toto, the owner and friend to Eva Longoria. In fact, I already had. Aside from my French lesson, I had bloodied a toe in my Jimmy Choos racing to get on the road.

I spotted Toto immediately. He was strikingly blonde, one of few I'd seen in Paris, and dressed in a crisp, button down shirt, fitted pants, and expensive French shoes. He stood in perfect form, leaning against the bar like he owned it. I mean, he did own it. Toto had his territory marked.

He hadn't seen me yet. I watched as he checked the time with a preoccupied glance and his brow crinkled. In that moment, I knew Toto was used to having his way. His powerful presence was disarming. Still, he was too old to be my type, although not any less attractive than men far younger, with his deep blue eyes and lean muscled body. Woof.

My ruby red-soled slippers clitter-clattered as I rushed toward him. I felt my nerves tighten and my stomach twirl. The adrenaline began pumping—for as many times as I'd been late, I still hate disappointing people, especially attractive older men.

"Toto, *Je suis désolé!*"

He looked up, and I saw the frustration visibly fade into puppy dog eyes. My work was done! My nerves immediately calmed when, with a poised *bonsoir,* he kissed cheek number one, then cheek number 2, while I repeated my new French phrase throughout. And then in English, "I'm sorry, I didn't realize we had a firm time. I thought you'd be here all night and you just meant for me to drop in, and then I...."

My long-winded explanation and nervous energy were cut short as Toto laughed.

"Drink. What do you want?"

French men don't waste time.

"Hmmm. I don't know. You pick for me!" His piercing blue eyes were distracting.

"Peach Martini. You didn't remember I owned this place? I do not work here."

"Well, I just assumed...."

"We will drink here and then go to meet my friends at my other restaurant—since we are off to a late start. Yes, okay?"

"Uh, ok. You own another restaurant?"

I'm not good with surprises—well, with men anyway. New men. Especially new French men, given how many of them had harassed me since I'd been in town. But perhaps this night I didn't have to keep such a short leash. Why not let Eva's dashing Toto take the lead? I sipped my drink and sputtered my new French phrase again and we both laughed and chatted on. Flirtation came as readily as the peach martini.

136

"Your friends were right. You speak English better than them!"

"Oh, my friends told you this?" Toto's eyebrow raised. He played it cool but clearly enjoyed the compliment. Meanwhile I wondered what his friends had in mind.

I told him about my dinner the night before with the lively group and before I could even finish my drink, he was ushering me out the door.

"Let's go! We'll take my scooter."

"What?" I stopped at this mention of scooter.

"Come on. It's safe and we aren't going far." I downed the martini and followed him outside to where his scooter was parked in front. Toto smiled at me, watching to see my reaction as he pulled out the most ridiculous helmet I'd ever seen. It looked like a prop from the Austin Powers films—pink with white flowers.

I'm not normally the girl who jumps on the back of a scooter with someone I've just met, especially in a foreign country. But what else was I going to do, say, "I don't do scooters, I'll meet you there?" I really couldn't handle more cobblestones and cabs in my stilettos. And besides, this Toto was a whole different breed. Older, attractive, funny, and full of surprises.

And so I went.

For the next eight minutes, I felt like I was atop that big dog in "The Neverending Story," flying through the streets of Paris. Exhilarated, I was reminded that at every turn on this trip, I was making my own luck. I closed my eyes and drank in the moment, feeling like we were flying above the clouds, the wind cool on my face.

We pulled up rock star style to an outside table at Peres et Filles, Toto's second restaurant. I clung to Toto as our scooter came to a swift halt. I immediately recognized Toto's partner RJ from my first trip to La Plage. He sat at a small café table with another man of about the same age, and they were laughing as they waved us in. We pulled off our helmets and his grin widened as we walked the few steps over to our table just feet from the vehicle. I felt all eyes on us, as if the whole restaurant was watching. My cheeks burned with the excitement of rolling in on the scooter as Toto's date. I love a grand entrance, even if my helmet was hot pink.

Toto seemed ever more relaxed with his friends as we said our hellos. RJ and I got reacquainted and he introduced me to Jason, their friend in from New York. I sat down with them while thinking about how I wanted the night to play out. I decided I'd have a nice drink with Toto, hear about his life, and then head off at a safe hour to see my friend and host, Jen.

My thoughts were interrupted as our waiter nervously hurried over to ask our order. His eyes focused on Toto. It reminded me of my junior year in college when I waitressed at Rande Gerber's Lemon Bar in NYC. My second week on the job, Rande came in to eat with a friend, and I could barely breathe every time I approached the table of the attractive mogul.

HOTEL COSTES

THE DESIGN MAXIM OF THE HOTEL COSTES WAS "ALL THINGS IN EXCESS," AND THIS BOUTIQUE HOTEL, ONE OF FRANCE'S FIRST, IS NOW RENOWNED AS A DEN OF OPULENCE. THE PROJECT PROPELLED ARCHITECT AND DECORATOR JACQUES GARCIA TO INTERNATIONAL FAME, AND HE HAS SINCE TRANSFORMED HOTELS AROUND THE WORLD AND DESIGNED A PRIVATE APARTMENT IN PARIS FOR THE SULTAN OF BRUNEI. ACCORDING TO *THE LUXURY TRAVEL BIBLE*, "GARCIA'S SIGNATURE STYLE IS AN EXOTIC MIX OF 17TH AND 18TH CENTURY REFERENCES BASED UPON HIS FRENCH HERITAGE. HE IS A PERFECTIONIST WHO TAKES TIME OVER THE SMALLEST TOUCHES. OPULENCE IS A KEYWORD.... GARCIA'S HOME, CHATEAU DU CHAMP DE BATAILLE, HAS EIGHTEEN LAVISHLY DECORATED BEDROOMS." "I WANTED PEOPLE TO FEEL THE WAY I FEEL AT HOME," HE HAS SAID OF HIS DECISION TO BECOME A HOTELIER. GIVEN THAT HIS HOME IS A CASTLE, GARCIA-DESIGNED PROPERTIES ARE QUITE THE EXPERIENCE.

Angie, in Paris go to hotel costes and have lunch and visit the pool it's amazing.

Also visit the store Collette which is close by—like a Fred segal, really cool books clothes etc. Good experience. Have crepes, they are the best. I will try and remember where the crepe place is but they're all great. The Louvre of course to see Mona Lisa.

In Amsterdam I will leave that for you to figure out but ??? Lol . But there are very cool shops along the river.

Barcelona, go to Gaudi park. he has amazing buildings and parks, it's a one of kind.

Rome, very touristy. First time you'll have to do the tourist stuff, the coliseum the fountain, the stairs etc. Hotel Boscolo is great to have a drink, it overlooks the center.

London, Ellen said go to topshop. Really cool clothes that are inexpensive like h&m but much cooler. London is so expensive so you'll love top shop to get some London style. Go to Hakasan, Asian food, amazing. Piccadilly, go to Dover St. It's really cool, just don't bring your wallet. Go to the top floor for tea. Go to Momo's for dinner and drinks or just drinks - we love momo's.

I will try and give you more places as I remember. Have a great time,

Chris and Ellen

I saw the same in this young man. He was intimidated as Toto smiled kindly and knowingly ordered another bottle of rosé, french fries, and something else French—all while pouring rosé into the empty wine glass in front of me. I had drowned out any words at this point, swept up in Toto's command of the situation. I had fallen back into cocktail waitress shoes and realized I was holding my breath.

His friends set me at ease, making sure I was comfortable—arranging my seat, offering me food, and then a smoke. I hadn't really been able to master the smoke in Paris, or ever for that matter. But I wanted to try. That's what was done in Paris, in chic cafés with bottomless glasses of rosé. So I took what was offered. That peach martini and scooter ride had me raring to go.

While Toto and RJ talked work, I bonded with their childhood friend, Jason, who was married with a new baby at home in New York—which helped me feel more wholesome as I puffed on the thin cigarette. He leaned over the small café table to explain the Parisian business talk in simple terms to me.

After another bottle of wine and another half cigarette (I still wasn't really getting it), Jason threw out to the group, "Why don't we change up the scene and have a drink at my hotel?"

"Where do you stay here in Paris?" I asked, excited for a new destination.

"Hotel le Costes."

I felt my eyes pop. "I am dying to go there! I had so many people mention it to me." Another Angie OMG moment ensued—here was my surprise chance to visit Ellen Pompeo and Chris Ivery's pick.

Toto laughed. "I think we need to take Angie for a drink at the hotel."

Like a child I jumped up, clapping my hands. "Woohoo!" I glanced over at Toto, hoping I wasn't embarrassing him, but his smile just lit me up even more. Another scooter ride!

The men laughed and Jason turned to me with the look of one of my brothers, a look that said, "You're really 30 going on 13!"

A quick scoot away and we pulled up to the hotel and walked into the lobby. I was mesmerized. It was so French—everything from the dimmed lighting in the lobby to the bright red umbrellas on the terrace to the cushiony deep red surrounding us. It was all très chic and very Paris. Toto and his crew glided easily through it all, clearly in their element.

First we sat outside with all the French hipsters, smoking cigarettes and drinking wine, talking and laughing. And then, we headed for the pinnacle of my Hotel Costes fantasy, the penthouse. Never did I imagine this happening without having to pay a lavish fee for entrance. My excitement escalated as the elevator shot past one floor after another.

The doors opened, and I stepped into the gorgeous four-room suite, set like a scene from an Anne Rice novel, or the kind of erotic thriller high school girls read behind closed doors. The classic, antique décor was bathed in rich reds, draped in velvet curtains, and accented by an orange glow. I skipped from room-to-room exploring every crevice, enjoying my escapade with the cool kids.

The men chatted, not paying much attention to my child-like enthusiasm, making it easier for me to take in my surroundings. I did find myself frequently under Toto's gaze, and gave as good as I got.

The conversation became background buzz and I grabbed the remote and flipped on MTV Paris. Ne-Yo's familiar gentlemanly face appeared. I felt a surge of excitement, having so recently spent the weekend dancing with him. I took a running start and dove onto the guest bed like a first grader, jumping up to dance. (More rosé, Angie?) Mid-jump I looked over and I saw that Jason was rolling a joint. Toto motioned to see if I wanted to smoke. Apprehensive, my eyes widened. I wasn't faking innocence—I didn't even know what pot was in high school and even now I was still no pro.

Confession: I'm pretty sure I ended up sampling the grass in every country I visited.

Shortly after it was *au revoir* to Jason and the penthouse. Toto and I scooted off to meet my friend Jen at Cabaret, a nightclub that was known for having the strictest door in Paris. Toto pulled the scooter right up to the velvet rope—apparently his confidence wasn't confined to his own restaurants.

No way, he's not getting away with this. The place is swarming with people wanting in! Toto seemed oblivious to these commoners. He also seemed too old to be the club type, so I tried to take over, pushing us through the crowd of young French hipsters, mostly male. This drill was second nature as I texted Jen to come get us. Before she could even respond, the bouncers saw Toto and to my surprise, led us in past the crowds. He didn't act as though he expected it at all, which made him even more attractive.

Despite my resolution to pass on the French men and their kisses while in Paris, I found myself wondering what might happen with Toto as the night went on.

We walked down the stairs, checked our coats, and set off to find Jen. The music was loud and the place was crowded. Toto took my hand as we made our way through different rooms. I felt myself swaying with the rosé and pot, yet I still felt in control. I found that while traveling, I always knew when to stop.

Cabaret was an underground space full of surprises. First, there was a cave-like room with a long bar and house music, then a private alcove complete with a corner pub and a funkier beat. I felt a tap on my shoulder, and turned to see Jen as she grabbed me in a big hug. She'd found us first and over the music yelled, "follow me," as she led us to the VIP area.

At the table, Jen, immediately suspicious of Toto, not-so-subtly pushed me toward an attractive 25-year-old Brazilian whose mischievous chiseled grin made me swoon. Or maybe it was the wine. Or the joint. Jen had been artfully plugging his arrival all day. He was the son of her close friend, the editor in chief at *Vogue* Brazil. He looked the part—stylish and preppy with just enough edge, and actually exactly my type. T-shirt tight across his broad chest, pleated pants that hung from his hips just right, hair perfectly coifed, skin taut and tanned, big gorgeous smile.

I had decided to pass on the French…but what about Brazilians in France?

He confidently took my hand in his and guided me closer. Swoon.

Then he opened his mouth: Paris, we have a problem. The club was loud, I was tipsy, and his English was not so great. But staring into his deep, dark eyes, I just kept talking, hoping that the near total lack of comprehension would work to flirtatious effect. I think we might have talked at each other for 20 minutes. All I got out of it was a really close examination of that dreamy chin, eyes, and the rest.

What about Toto? Poor Toto. He held his own on the other side of the booth, but Jen had obviously not warmed to him at all. And here I was rewarding his kind treatment of me all night by making googley eyes with the Brazilian. Suddenly something snapped, and I realized I was getting drunk. It was time for Angie to go home and put herself to bed.

I backed away from the Brazilian and pulled Jen close.

"Exhausted. Getting cab. Need bed." Did I mention pot makes me sleepy? No one was getting kissed this night.

I said goodbye to Brazil and told Toto I had to go home. I should have guessed that he'd offer to take me. I politely declined, not wanting to impose and remembering my vow. Of course, he insisted and followed me out, so I had no choice but to accept. The whole ride home, inside that pink flowered helmet, I was having a war of two Angies, one who was worrying about how to fend off Toto's inevitable advances, the other puckering her lips in preparation. This second Angie was an Angie I knew well in Europe: The Kissing Bandit (TKB). She always came

BIO ▼

ELLEN POMPEO

Ellen Pompeo was named TV's highest paid actress, a veteran on "Grey's Anatomy." She is exactly the kind of mom I want to be, the "have baby, will travel" kind. She and her music producer husband Chris Ivery brought their baby, Stella, to Oakley's Learn to Drive racecar driving event, and they were the perfect team. She once told *People* that since she's had Stella, "Every day has been like Christmas morning."

out after a few rosés. One thing was sure, I didn't want to screw up a friendship with one of the few Frenchies I had liked so far.

Toto pulled up to Jen's apartment and turned to me, pulling off my helmet. I felt a sharp intake of breath. Was it the fresh air or was I feeling the romance of France? The Eiffel Tower hovered, the moonlight hinted at shadowy objects on the street, and our faces were close as the motor came to a quiet halt. I started to thank Toto, raising my eyes. And as soon as ours met, he leaned in to kiss me. TKB took over, loving it. Straddling the motorcycle, regular Angie was sensing a point of no return. Toto's kiss was intoxicating. I pulled away, shaking my tipsy head straight, and removed myself from the bike.

"Come back with me," he said. "I promise you I'll be good."

"I'm so sorry. I must go to bed…alone. I'm exhausted."

"Promise you'll come to brunch tomorrow!"

"Of course."

And he pulled away.

I walked, even glided, toward Jen's, buoyed by a fizzy feeling of accomplishment. I may have even air-pumped. I had stood my ground with Toto and managed not to do anything stupid with the gorgeous Brazilian *Vogue* editor's son. I needed some kind of award. Maybe this would help move forward my VIP Vatican tour request, which was still unan-swered. "She resisted a restaurateur and a Brazilian? *Mio Dio*! Special viewing with the Pope!"

And then I saw him. From behind the glare of headlights, a cute, floppy-haired boy had stumbled out of the backseat of a cab. Young-pants. I watched him almost fall, obviously drunk. He looked up at me and said hello. Oh no you don't. I felt TKB stir.

We walked together, chatting under the glimmer of the moon and the streetlights. Cut to an hour later, TKB was pushing her new friend against an elevator wall as he pressed PH.

Six hours later, I groggily lifted my head. Next to me was that irresist-ible (eh?) shaggy head. I took in the rest of the scene. All around the room were model airplanes. We were sleeping on "Star Wars" sheets.

Dear lord, what had I done?

I couldn't sit still a minute longer. With a cringe, I peeled back his shaggy locks. "Wake up! Wake up! How old are you, anyway?" I threw back the sheets, and was incredibly relieved to discover I was fully dressed. I was still mortified, but at least now I could be sure that no crime had been committed.

"Shhhh!" he said, waking up to slowly to answer my question.

Surprised at being shushed, I asked if he had roommates.

He shrugged. "Sorta."

"Can I have water, please?"

He left to get it, and I took the chance to look more closely around the room. Pilot figurines. Textbooks. This picture was not improving. Kissing Bandit, shame on you. What was wrong with me? I had been so good!

Returning with the water, Youngpants seemed…well, young. I chat-ted him up about Paris. "Which way is the bathroom?" I finally asked, hoping to sleuth a bit more before departing.

"Well…not yet."

"Why not?" I stood up, heading for the hall.

Youngpants yanked me back—and not in a gentle, controlled way. Total panic.

"Uh, you can't."

Wait for it, wait for it…

"My parents are here."

Yeah, I'd never get into the Vatican.

"What?? You live with your parents?" I groaned, wishing I could turn into one of his tiny green pilot figurines and fly away.

"Well yeah, not for long, you know, just in between. I was in the states for school and just graduated."

I buried my head in the "Star Wars" pillows.

"High school?"

"No, aviation school."

I needed to get out, but now Youngpants wanted to share his life dreams.

"Yes, after aviation school in Florida, I wanted to have some time here before I decided if I wanted for sure to stay in the states. My parents said I could have this summer to figure out what I want to do with my life."

And so, like a school guidance counselor, I did what I had to. I sat there listening and offering up advice to this fine young fellow I had made out with in an elevator.

Finally we heard a door shut, signaling that his parents had left for work. I jumped up like a fuselage was under me. Today's session was definitely over.

On the walk home, I realized this was the ultimate Parisian finale. Later that day I was on a train to Barcelona. I smiled, and imagined myself back on a certain scooter with a hot blonde, with the wind in my face and the giddy rush of peach martini.

TRIPPING POINT

Be good, but not too good. It'll burn you every time.

QUICK HITS | PARIS

ROMANY MALCO | "WEEDS"

...The French are keen on open, confident, worldly souls and will not hesitate to flirt. ... **My favorite part of Paris is the 4th Arrondissement also known as Place de la Bastille. It is the closest thing Paris has to Brooklyn.** The moment you come out of the tube (train station) there is a modest Thai restaurant to your right on Rue Roquette that is delicious...

• •

GREG GRUNBERG | ACTOR, "HEROES"

...Elizabeth and I went backpacking through Europe before we had kids and one of the many things we remember was **our night under the tower watching Jean Michelle Jarre perform while sharing a blanket with thousands of other tourists and locals and taking in the spectacle that is Paris.** Also, you MUST eat at a little "steak & fries" place near the Four Season's hotel (George V)—ask the concierge to direct you...

• •

YVONNE STRAHOVSKI | "DEXTER"

...Paris is to die for. Favorite memory? **Eating a big fat baguette** with ham and cheese and having a coffee at a cafe under the Notre Dame...

• •

ZACH GILFORD | "FRIDAY NIGHT LIGHTS"

...Paris is an amazing walking city besides the obvious things to see, **make sure to visit the Rodin museum.** One of my favorites i have ever seen...

• •

MARISA COUGHLAN | "BOSTON LEGAL"

...I love a bar in Paris called Pub Saint Germain . . . we used to go there ALL the time in college and get REALLY drunk off these **crazy smoking drinks called the SCORPION.** I hate to only have an idea that involves huge amounts of alcohol, but we really had the best time putting those back and the bar is really cool and the area is amazing. Bring friends, you can't drink it alone! Near ODEON metro stop...

• •

AJ DIPERSIA | "HEMINGWAY"

...Paris is one of those cities where i like to do what i would do if i were at home. i like to smoke joints, walk through the park, check the museum if there's something cool going on, see a movie, eat some food, chill at a friend's house, go out. it's the best way to know paris. **just pretend you just moved there**...

• •

MILO VENTIMIGLIA | ACTOR, "HEROES"

...The best part of Paris is having someone to be in the city with. Otherwise the gloom and architecture of the city brings about a very lonely feel. People are kinda rude, or just "French," but I'm sure you'll meet some great people. **Staring at the Mona Lisa was kinda cool. Wondering in fact if it was the real one. There are seven, six fakes and one real...**

• •

HOLLY WIERSMA | PRODUCER, "BOBBY"

...Take the train to St. Tropez. It is the most beautiful place in the world. The beaches are amazing. Everyone goes to Club 55 which is a restaurant on the beach and then lays on the beach (top optional). You have a glass of rosé and nothing is better...

• •

MURRAY MILLER | PRODUCER, "GIRLS"

...I spent most of my time in Paris in **Montmartre–it's where they shot Amelie and really feels like cartoon Paris–people in berets riding bikes with baskets full of baguettes.** There's one main street with cafes and then a little town up by the church, Sacre Cour, built on top of a huge hill, you can't miss it...

• •

QUICK HITS | PARIS

. . . .

MOLLY SIMS | MODEL & ACTRESS

…Get tea in the Marriage des Freres …. you must get a gyro in the Marais as well. Also, if you visit a drugstore, **get Bourgois makeup. It is Chanel, just packaged cheaply…**

. . . .

PAGE FARMER | OWNER REGINA BARRETT

…Late winter 2010 on a last minute work trip to Paris by chance I stayed at a **cute boutique hotel designed by Philippe Starck called Mama Shelter.** To my surprise it was super hip, great staff and fun bar etc. only downside it was 15 minutes off the grid…

. . . .

Barcelona

CHAPTER 19 THE SPANISH ROADRUNNER

DESTINATION The Cava Bar, Barcelona

INSPIRATION Sommelier Palmer Emmitt sends me to a "shady little meat market/champagne distributer."

• • • • • • • • • • • • • • • • • • •

My first mission in Barcelona: find the Cava Bar. The spot was best described to me as a "shady little meat market/champagne distributer that is by far the most unique and fun place I've ever been anywhere in the world." Coming from Palmer Emmitt, one of my most well-traveled friends and a sommelier, this was a big moment. Did I mention Palmer had been to Barcelona 14 times?

The bar was down an alley, off the beaten path, dirty and raw but pulsing with an energy I wanted most to remember Barcelona by. Walking through the garage-like door that opened onto the street, I was in awe of the elaborate production. Meat hung from the ceiling, butchers pointed into the crowd, and sandwich makers smiled as they passed out orders, trusting patrons to pay for what they ordered. It was so crowded that even early in the evening the plastic champagne flutes couldn't be refilled fast enough to keep a close check. I couldn't imagine anyone stiffing them though, considering champagne was about a dollar a glass and sandwiches the same.

The place was full of travelers and locals and everyone stood around—within inches of one another—drinking and swapping stories. I enjoyed a long happy hour, and met interesting people with fascinating life stories, before deciding to walk back to the hotel. There was just enough light left in the sky for me to feel safe.

FROM Palmer Emmitt
TO   Angie Banicki
subject Re: 30 before 30

The big thing not to miss is Can Paixano, a.k.a The Cava Bar, a shady little meat market/champagne distributor that is by far the most unique and fun place I've ever been anywhere in the world. You also must spend a morning at the Sagrada Familia, the great Gaudi cathedral that has been under construction for the last 100 years, and hike to the top of one of the towers. It's the most beautiful and fascinating structure and it will change your life.

On the way back, I got caught up window-shopping, stopping at every street seller to examine their strands of colorful Spanish jewelry. By now it was dark, but I felt safe knowing there were people all around me. As I strolled along, my thoughts were on the Camino de Santiago, the 500-mile religious pilgrimage through Spain. The teachers I'd just met at Cava had been telling me about the walk—30 days, city through city, visiting historical and spiritual monuments, making friends young and old. One of the men I'd met had lived in Los Angeles and after the trek had given up his job and moved to Europe to continue his pursuit of spiritual truth.

Lost in thought, it all seemed to happen so quickly. He was a roadrunner—that little Spanish man bolted out of the alleyway and swooped right past me. I felt the swoosh from behind and instinctively held tight to my stuff. Every muscle taut throughout the "struggle." The rest was slow motion and partially blurred. The pickpocket's biggest mistake was grabbing for my BlackBerry. I held it in one hand, and my clutch in the other. That little thief could have had my cash and IDs for sure, but buddy, you messed with the wrong girl for a BlackBerry.

BIO ▶▶
PALMER EMMITT

I've known Palmer since I first moved to LA—we were part of a group of friends in our early 20s who were all figuring ourselves out. Today Palmer has his own business, Cellar Door Wine Consulting, and travels the world as a sommelier. He had wanted to find a way to travel for work and he made it happen, way before I did.

My arm whipped back and out came a loud, low scream-ish bark from deep down within me, in a place I didn't know existed—a transsexual buried inside who took over with his male *cojones*. It was a sound I'd never heard before and I felt 8 sets of eyes within 10 feet staring at me. Just watching me—pretending they hadn't seen or heard the interaction. Not one of the couples, tourists, or street vendors came to see if I was okay. I couldn't even be mad at them for not trying to save me, for I was mortified by the caveman unleashed from within. Just get home. Instead of searching their averting eyes for compassion or embarrassment for not acknowledging the violation, I looked down, holding back tears. Probably because I knew they were actually frightened by the beast inside me who showed his fearlessness in my moment of pain. I preferred indifference in the moment, but later I realized this was the genesis of my indifference to Barcelona.

TRIPPING POINT

Travel isn't always perfectly safe, but it's usually worth the risk. Sometimes you just have to grab life by the balls.

Back at the hotel, I snuck by the white desk at the entrance, not wanting to have to talk to anyone. I was pretty shaken up, but wasn't ready to admit it to myself or anyone else. Falling onto the bed in my room, I tried not to be a crybaby, but tears welled up beyond my control.

I had a fierce gorilla inside protecting me, with a growl so low, so primal, it made people run—run from fear of the freak within.

CAMINO DE SANTIAGO

EL CAMINO DE SANTIAGO IS THE PILGRIMAGE ROUTE TO THE CATHEDRAL OF SANTIAGO DE COMPOSTELA IN GALICIA IN NORTHWESTERN SPAIN, WHERE TRADITION HAS IT THAT THE REMAINS OF THE APOSTLE SAINT JAMES ARE BURIED. IN ENGLISH, IT IS CALLED THE WAY OF ST. JAMES AND IT HAS EXISTED FOR OVER 1,000 YEARS. TENS OF THOUSANDS OF CHRISTIAN PILGRIMS AND OTHER TRAVELERS SET OUT ON THIS PILGRIMAGE EACH YEAR. THE MOST POPULAR ROUTE, WHICH GETS VERY CROWDED IN MID-SUMMER, IS THE CAMINO FRANCES, WHICH STRETCHES NEARLY 500 MILES FROM ST. JEAN-PIED-DU-PORT NEAR BIARRITZ IN FRANCE TO SANTIAGO.

CHAPTER 20 BOHEMIAN BARCELONA

DESTINATION Ed Maklouf's hood

INSPIRATION Kevin Parker hooks me up with a guy who imports the world's craziest hats and we accidentally wander into a "happening."

● ● ● ● ● ● ● ● ● ● ● ● ● ● ● ● ● ● ● ●

From talking to my friend Kevin, I thought he sent me to meet his best buddy. But when Ed and I met in Barcelona, I got the real story.

"Kevin and I only met once, in London. I think it was at a late night party in a basement somewhere!"

That's the beauty of connection, though. It can happen in a moment. Ed became quite the character in my Barcelona story and has since become a friend for life. He's an entrepreneur and a risk taker, always with another new idea. He's the founder of a Barcelona startup called Siine, trying to build a better keyboard for intuitive texting. Ed later enthusiastically told me about his idea to import very strange, tall, striped cone-shaped hats. Ed was nothing like I could have imagined. He was a skinny white dude with long hippy hair—no Spaniard at all. When we met, he was nervous about making sure he provided a good moment for me. I tried to calm him down about it. "Meeting you, my friend's friend in Barcelona, is special enough!" But that just seemed to add more pressure.

When he learned where I had been so far—an exhilarating run through Guell Park high above the city, the Ritz Barcelona (where they named a gin cocktail after me)—he decided that it was time to take me off the beaten path.

"I'm going to take you to a restaurant on the Bohemian side of town," he told me. What crazy part of town we ended up in, I don't know. The restaurant was outside, and it didn't feel like a restaurant at all. It felt like friends cooking BBQ outside.

We had barely settled in when I noticed something happening. Maybe 30 feet away there was a blank wall, and two guys covering it in white paper.

Ed waved it off as nothing, but I said, "No, I think something's about to happen."

Sure enough, a guy got up and said in Spanish, very grandly, "I want to welcome you all here!" There were only about seven of us in the whole place.

We watched as the two artists both lit joints. Then they welcomed their parents to the event and made a little speech. Ed and I looked at each other, amazed.

Finally they started drawing. They drew huge circles, and then started filling them in. Walkers passed by the work-in-process. Were they part of the art? One man stopped, picked up chalk, and helped fill in one of the circles. The men patted his back and he walked on. They continued drawing.

Next they drew a little man, and the man's shadow, and connected it to the circle.

Was it abstract?

Hula hoops?

Worlds colliding?

I started to wish I was smoking the pot. People walking through the restaurant area were as confused as we were. Ed seemed embarrassed at this random, not all that impressive art show, but I loved that it was bizarre and fun and completely unexpected. It didn't have to be Gaudi—it was alive, and that was enough.

Ed was reluctant to engage with the artists, and even more reluctant when I wanted to get a picture. But I persisted and the artists were thrilled. Thanks to little American me, they now had an international audience for their work. I still have no idea what they were really up to, except that the circles were definitely worlds. But their enthusiasm was so contagious that even Ed opened up to it.

BIO

KEVIN PARKER

Talent manager (Rain Management Group) and TV producer Kevin Parker seems to have the special gift of being omnipresent. He's been a staple at every birthday party, every award season event, every Sundance shindig I've gone to for years. I don't know how he does it, but it's impressive, and that's coming from a professional goer-outer herself.

TRIPPING POINT

Art is most fun when it's least pretentious. Shift your attention to the artist, and let their enthusiasm carry you.

Angie,

Here's old itinerary from a trip to Barcelona that has a bunch of info on it. Also, contact my buddy Ed Maklouf when you get to Barcelona, he's one of the most interesting guys I've met.
KP

The bus turistica seems a little cheesy, but it is actually a great way to see the city and go to all of the big tourist attractions. You can hop on and off at anytime, so it is a good way to maximize your time in getting to the main sites.

Make sure you see as much of gaudi's work as possible. Parque Guell is my personal favorite, and casa mila and casa battlo are also worth a trip. I'm sure you will check out las ramblas, but off of the strip are barrio gotico and the latin quarter, which are cool neighborhoods to walk around. Also off of las ramblas is la boqueria, which is a huge outdoor market. There are a few restaurants in there (think outdoor diners) that have some great tapas. Porto olympico is pretty touristy, but near the water if you want to walk around. The picasso museum is cool.

If you can go to a soccer game, definitely do it. FC barcelona (barca) is one of the proudest and most famous clubs in europe and their stadium holds over 100,000. This is a religious experience. If they are not playing espanyol is the other team in town (like the mets to barca's yankees).

I know you said you wanted to go to/near the beach. Sitges is a little artsy town that is a 35 minute train ride from barcelona. They have a film festival in the fall, and it is a pretty relaxed place.

CHAPTER 21 OSCAR THE FRIENDLY GROUCH

DESTINATION The Pipe Club, Barcelona

INSPIRATION Former NBC President Ben Silverman says I should find a hot Spaniard to take me for drinks after seeing Gaudi's work—but it doesn't exactly work out that way.

• • • • • • • • • • • • • • • • • • •

Oscar, a friend of a friend, had promised to take me to a secret spot in Barcelona. Having not yet found Ben Silverman's hot Spaniard for drinks, I had high hopes for our date. He turned out to be slightly older, slightly portly, and slightly homely–not the most attractive guy I ever met, but he did give me a huge grin that set me at ease. The awkward hug he gave me upon meeting, less successful. No biggle. His eyes twinkled and I couldn't help myself, I twinkled right back. As he took my arm and led me across the square, an enthusiastic tour guide, I smiled, thinking that we were quite the couple: In my wedges I stood a good foot above Oscar.

And yet I felt comfortable with this short, balding sweet man.

Just a few blocks away and in no hurry, with only the intention of getting to know each other, we walked and talked about Barcelona, especially the Sagrada Familia, Gaudi's great masterpiece of a church and Barcelona's most famous attraction. Oscar explained that construction had begun in the 1800s, and they still weren't finished. It was only in 2010 that they even started holding services there.

I asked Oscar about his job and life in Barcelona. That was the first moment I realized that his English wasn't great, now that he was talking about something outside of the guidebooks. But we managed alright. He still lived with his parents–I found this not to be uncommon throughout Europe. If you were still single, it was considered okay. I judged him a little bit anyway, and then felt judged myself: Dear God, had our mutual friends thought that we could be an item?

The secret spot was called the Pipe Club in Reial Square, next to Las Ramblas. The Square is lined with dance clubs, and sometimes there are flamenco performances right on the street. On that night, and on the early side, it was quieter. Pipe Club was in a far corner. Oscar had already let me know that you had to be invited or be a member to get in. As we approached the nondescript door, I had the feeling I'd be frisked or quizzed, but no—just a smile from the man in shadow so dark I had only a slanted top hat to remember him by. He pointed, and we entered the grey steel elevator. Something told me no tourists would be on the other side.

The contrast between the steely grey elevator and what I saw as the doors opened could not have been more extreme. We walked into a room that looked like an opulent set from "Eyes Wide Shut," except everyone had their clothes on and the masks were Spanish style and on the walls, not on people's faces. (Actually, as I came to discover, the bar has a Sherlock Holmes theme.) The bar swam in an orange hue and the music was loud Spanish jazz that made me want to jump on the bar to dance. Old men smoking cigars and pipes sat at tables with patrons who seemed to gather in this "local" watering hole regularly.

Oscar seemed just as excited to show me the place as I was to see it, and led me to two bar stools cramped in the corner facing the bar.

"Whiskey, *por favor*," he told the bartender. I had the same, wanting to do as the old-men locals do. We smoked cigars and shared stories. Oscar was very much a gentleman. He encouraged me with smiles and nodding. Talking to him was easy, although I suspected that his rapt interest in my every word was mostly because he didn't get out of his parents' house much.

As I downed my whiskey, my BlackBerry was buzzing with emails from several other new friends, all men, who all seemed to be expect-

THE BARCELONA PIPE CLUB

THE BARCELONA PIPA CLUB (THE BARCELONA PIPE CLUB) DATES BACK TO 1962, AND TODAY HAS UPWARDS OF 400 MEMBERS. HIDDEN IN A THIRD FLOOR APARTMENT, THIS SHERLOCK HOLMES-THEMED CLUB FOR PIPE AFICIONADOS WELCOMES NON-SMOKERS TOO. THEIR WEBSITE INFORMS YOU THAT YOU'LL RECEIVE "A WARM WELCOME: THERE'S ROOM FOR EVERYONE AND IT'S EASY TO FIND SOMETHING TO YOUR LIKING—FRIENDSHIP, CONVERSATION, DRINKS, LIVE JAZZ, GASTRONOMIC SAMPLING, OR A SUPERB MEAL—PART OF LIFE'S SMALL PLEASURES AND THE CLUB'S PHILOSOPHY." UNLIKE OTHER BARS IN BARCELONA, PIPA CLUB'S STATUS AS A MEMBERS-ONLY VENUE ALLOWS IT TO STAY OPEN PAST 3 A.M., MAKING IT ONE OF THE MOST COLORFUL LATE-NIGHT SCENES IN THE CITY.

ing me to meet them that night. My reaction was unusual: Total emotional overwhelm. It was the whiskey talking, somewhat, but more I think it was still the after-effect of being mugged my first night in town. I still hadn't talked to anyone about it. And now, here, surrounded by well-dressed old men and clouds of cigar smoke, it was all coming out. Tears began to form.

Oscar immediately asked if I was okay and I tried to explain the emails and all that had happened—how I was feeling threatened, no longer able to trust my instincts with people or places, scared by all these new acquaintances. Oscar listened carefully, nodding seriously at times, giving me plenty of space and gazing at me with understanding eyes.

After a rush of words and waterworks, I felt better. Oscar patted my hair in a kind, fatherly gesture, and said he'd walk me home, if I wanted to go. I smiled through my few re-

maining tears and suggested we finish our whiskeys and then go. Oscar walked me back and at the foot of my hotel, I gave him a big hug and then a long thank you—for his kindness, his gentlemanliness, his willingness to listen with no agenda.

I was midway through the speech, probably my most earnest ever, when he grabbed my head, pulled my face in, and gave me the world's most slobbery kiss. I jerked back: "What are you doing?!" Oscar seemed totally shocked at my response, a little angry even, but mostly confused. Very confused.

And that's when I realized the truth of sweet, gentle, English-deprived Oscar: He had barely understood a word I said the entire night.

I could have been upset, but instead I just had to laugh. I had gotten him all wrong, but it didn't matter. The crying had served its purpose, and I felt myself getting better, stronger, and back to myself.

FROM Ben Silverman
TO Angie Banicki

You must read a moveable feast which is one of Hemmingway's best books and a love affair to Paris, u must then go to St. Surplice in Paris and sit at its fountain and have a kir vin blanc or kir royal if u prefer champagne and read a page or two of the book at the café there. Another amazing memory is walking through the ile de Saint Louis via l'eglise Nortre Dame and getting ice cream at berthillion. In Barcelona you must walk the ramblas all the way north and see the Gaudi architecture which made the city so alive and then find a nice hot Spaniard to buy you a sangria and some tapas and then to find an absinthe bar.

TRIPPING POINT

Most people hear what they want to—add in a language barrier and what do you get? Slobbered on.

QUICK HITS | BARCELONA

DAVID BUGLIARI | AGENT, CAA

...In Barcelona....**anyone and everyone will want to speak with you**.... it's a huge European destination city...and it never sleeps. Clubs don't even open until after midnight....it's insane....make sure you hydrate!!!...

• •

ALAN POLSKY | PRODUCER

...**Make sure to see the Gaudi architecture, and don't go out before 1 a.m.....**

• •

COURTNEY REUM | FOUNDER, VEEV

...I would recommend you rent some type of vespa/scooter. Make sure you **eat tapas throughout the day and just go up and down the main drag (La Rambla).** Literally, if you just wander around there you will see so many interesting things, people and conversations...once Spaniards finish their siestas they just sit outside and chat/hang out until the wee hours and I've never seen anything quite like it...

• •

MIKE ROSENTHAL | PHOTOGRAPHER

...My favorite thing was **the bike tour I took. I got to see the best parts of the city, in a way I'd normally never get to experience**. I highly recommend going to a sports bar to watch the soccer games. Even if you aren't a fan, and know nothing about futbol, the energy and enthusiasm is unmatched by anything we have here...

• •

CELINE KHAZARANI | PRADA

...Go to the **cactus garden on Montjuic Hill.** It's magical and unreal...

• •

JAMIE LYNN SIGLER | ACTRESS, "SOPRANOS"

...Our fav night was walking around the artist district, grabbing a bite at Cal Pep at 11 p.m. and walking around **drinking $1 beers until 3 a.m.** Best trip of my life...

• •

Rome

CHAPTER 22 GRAPE ESCAPES

DESTINATION Villa Geggiano Vineyard, Siena

INSPIRATION Wine enthusiast, author, and entrepreneur
Gary Vaynerchuck sends me "on the finest wine tour the Italians can
provide."

• • • • • • • • • • • • • • • • • • •

After five years of talking about wanting to go to Italy, my parents
had booked a trip—their first international voyage—and within just one
month of hearing that their daughter was going. This was the most
spontaneous move I'd ever seen my parents, the conservative anti-risk-
takers, make. I had no idea how much I would need and appreciate
them being there until I sat on the train ride from Rome to Florence
to meet them. Emotions were bubbling up like sparkling wine poured
straight from the bottle—fizzing in the mouth, down the throat, and then
seeping back up, reminding me not to rush. I was yearning for some
parental love.

I would have just one day with my parents in Italy, and I'd decided
we would spend it near Siena, on the wine tour Gary V had arranged.
My parents, however, would have been happier to stay in Florence,
where they had booked a hotel that looked like Austin Powers and
Lady Gaga had teamed up to design it, complete with bright colored
walls and furry furniture, and to my dad's great glee (which he didn't
hold back from exclaiming to everyone), a bidet. It took me telling them
I had gotten a refund for their last night and secretly paying for their
room to get them out of there and on the Angie adventure train.

Once on board, I was anxious, because I had dragged them away
and now couldn't tell them much about what to expect. All I really knew
was that a man named Andrea would be showing us around a vineyard

called Geggiano. Our cabbie got lost twice in the three-mile trip from our hotel to the vineyard.

"Guys, I don't really know what we are getting into, but that's the beauty of it."

I tried to be convincing, but truthfully I was nervous right up until the moment we stepped out of the cab, and the enchanting hills of the Chianti Classico region—world-famous for its wines, its natural beauty, and its quiet farmhouses—were finally before us.

A man in his early 50s came out. He could've been a Banicki, with his lean figure and light graying hair. He was timid, seemingly as unsure of the situation as we were, but his eyes were kind. I went straight into Angie Banicki event mode.

"Are you Andrea? Hi, I'm Angie Banicki! Thank you so much again for having us! I brought my parents along for the visit. This is Guy and another Andrea."

We all shook hands and stood at the gate, making small talk. We put together the pieces of how we'd been connected. Funnily enough, Andrea had never even met Gary. I loved hearing that I'd been brought here in a sort of connect-the-dots kind of way. We were still unsure of who Andrea was—vineyard keeper, gardener, wine enthusiast like Gary? Andrea's warm smile gave away nothing.

"Now where would you like to start? Do you want a tour? Or a wine

172

VILLA DI GEGGIANO

THE BROTHERS WHO RUN THIS ESTATE BOAST A GRAND VILLA JUST OUTSIDE SIENA, A POPE IN THE FAMILY, THREE LAST NAMES, AND SOME OF THE BEST CHIANTI CLASSICO ON THE MARKET TODAY. ANDREA AND ALESSANDRO BOSCU BIANCHI BANDINELLI ARE THE CURRENT PROPRIETORS OF THE VILLA DI GEGGIANO, A NATIONAL MONUMENT THAT HAS BEEN IN THEIR FAMILY SINCE 1527; DOCUMENTS SHOW THAT THE FAMILY WAS ALREADY PRODUCING WINE HERE AND EXPORTING IT TO GREAT BRITAIN IN 1725. ORIGINALLY THE FAMILY'S SUMMER HOUSE, THE VILLA STILL TOUTS ITS 18TH-CENTURY DÉCOR AND FURNISHINGS, AND THE FAMILY IS PROUD TO TELL OF THE FAMOUS GUESTS WHO HAVE GRACED THESE ROOMS. TODAY THE ESTATE COVERS 20 HECTARES, ENCOMPASSING THE FORMAL OUTDOOR THEATER THAT IS STILL USED IN THE SUMMER, A TANTALIZING VEGETABLE GARDEN, AND GROUNDS THAT INCLUDE ABOUT 8 HECTARES OF VINEYARDS. IN THE CELLAR OF THE VILLA, APPROXIMATELY 40,000 BOTTLES OF PREMIUM CHIANTI CLASSICO AND RED TUSCAN IGT WINES ARE PRODUCED EACH YEAR, FOLLOWING THE HIGHEST QUALITY CRITERIA AND SOLD TO SEVERAL INTERNATIONAL GOURMET SHOPS, RESTAURANTS, AND HOTELS.

tasting? Do you want to see the grounds?"

"Wine! We want the wine!" chimed my father. Guy Banicki is always up for a drink. I waved him away.

"Andrea—we want it all! This is your moment for us. We want you to show us what you think we'll like. We are just so grateful to be here."

Andrea suggested we started with a walk around the grounds. Mom headed straight to the gardens, where she and Andrea dropped names of plants and flowers that were foreign to me. This was my mother's idea of heaven. Behind the house, the luscious greens had been trimmed into an arch, creating the stage for an outdoor theater.

Dad and I looked out at the vineyards and looked at each other in curious awe. "Does he own all this?" Dad said it aloud. I shrugged. "I have no idea, but I have a feeling we will find out."

Mom and Andrea sauntered back over to Dad and me,

laughing and comfortable. "Guy, they have azaleas in the garden! I've got to get some for our yard!"

Andrea explained that theirs was one of the smaller Chianti vineyards. They turn out 40,000 bottles a year, compared to a big producer who might bottle 2 million. He told us how difficult it was, the tremendous amount of physical upkeep just to maintain the grounds. His vineyard maintains a small distribution to restaurants in Siena, and just a few others abroad, including the likes of Wolfgang Puck.

I asked about the tiny house that sat on the edge of the grounds.

Andrea shrugged modestly as he led us to it. "Back in the day these were the maid's quarters. I decided it would be a fun project to recreate it as a honeymoon suite for couples who were married here in the vineyard." It was starting to become clear that this was Andrea's home, although he still hadn't said so.

He opened the door to the small cottage, revealing an oasis of bamboo, with a ceiling made of the same that opened up to allow the night sky in. I snuck off to explore the nooks and crannies while my parents ooh-ed and aah-ed.

"This artistic detail is incredible! How did you come up with the lighting structure and the skylight plan?" Mom was incredulous. Andrea blushed.

As we headed back to the main house, Andrea Bianchi Bandinelli began to open up. The vineyard had been in their family since the 16th century. When their mother grew too old to maintain it, the city offered to buy it to turn it into a museum. He and his brothers struggled with the decision: Keep it or sell it? Selling it would mean that they could move their families to Rome and pursue other passions.

Ultimately, they found a way to do both, but it had been a struggle. Andrea had married and raised two kids in Rome, where he became an architect. He and his brother came back to help their mother as often as they could. But now that his children had grown, he spent more of his time on the vineyard. He gardens himself, even though they have groundskeepers, and he travels to sell the wine. His brother Alessandro minds the vineyards and cellar.

Back inside the main house, in the library, Andrea walked us through framed portraits of members of his family going back to the 1700s. Mom, ever the librarian, focused on the books, and found one with Andrea's last name on the cover.

"Wait, I know this book!"

"Yes, that was my father's…it was very important to him," Andrea explained.

"This is a well-regarded history of Italian art," Mom exclaimed. She held it up to show me, her eyes wide. We could see that Andrea was proud. His father was a well-regarded Marxist art historian and archeologist who also wrote a memoir of Italy under fascism, published after his death. As a professor at the University of Florence, he had been assigned the task of giving a tour of Italy's finest classical objects to Hitler and Mussolini, but by the time he was asked to do the same for Hermann Goering, he had turned to communism, in disgust with fascism. He refused to give the tour. In his later years, he had devoted himself entirely to archeology and art, living at the Villa Geggiano.

Time to try the wine. Anticipating that first sip, Dad Banicki rubbed his hands and clapped in anticipation—a gesture I recognized as one of my own. Some people have centuries-old villas as their family legacy. I have hand clapping.

After spending almost three hours at the villa—three times what Andrea had said he intended to spend with us—our host had become a new friend.

As we sat sampling wine and eating goodies, my parents shared that this had been without a doubt the best part of their trip to Italy, thanking Andrea over and over. He then offered to drive us back into town for our dinner. We started to refuse, but I could see in his eyes that he was looking for a way to extend his time with us.

On that drive back, Andrea shared a special story from his youth that Mom Banicki later said he purposely saved until the end. "Our principal at school always said kids save the most important thing for last. They leave you with the nugget they want you to remember most."

Andrea described his most cherished travel memory. As a college student, he and his brothers had taken their first trip together to the United States. They went with little money and much adventurous spirit. They bought a junky old Volkswagen van, these five Italian brothers, and traveled from New York to California. But they almost didn't make it. Fifty miles outside of California, where food and a place to stay awaited them, their car broke down. They had run out of money. Not knowing what to do, they knocked on a stranger's door. The woman there took them in for the night and fed them in exchange for a few household repairs. The next day they managed to get their van going and made it to the sunny shores of California.

It wasn't just the details he shared—you could see him reliving the emotions, the intense appreciation of that time with his brothers and the memory of how the trip had changed him. His story touched my soul, and my parents' too. Immediately I recognized that this journey, this day for my parents and me, would be that kind of memory, if we continued to relax and feel it.

We left Andrea's company intoxicated, but not by the wine. Well, not only by the wine.

Later I got this email:

Dear Angie,

Thank you very much for your kind email. I was so pleased to meet you and your parents, the time that we have spent together was a true pleasure for me too.

I couldn't expect a better birthday gift. (Yes, the day we met I became a little bit older).

Ciao,
Andrea

BIO▶▶

GARY VAYNERCHUCK

Online marketing trailblazer Gary Vaynerchuk is a 33-year-old entrepreneur whose dual identity as both business guru and wine guy has made him known as the "Social Media Sommelier." I got to know him through my friend Palmer, who's also in this book. Palmer, a sommelier himself, was watching "Gary's Wine Library TV" show (affectionately known as "The Thunder Show") before anyone else. Today he's the author of two *New York Times* business best-sellers, *Crush It* and *The Thank You Economy*, but his ambition doesn't stop there: His ultimate goal is to own the New York Jets. Finally, though his various businesses obviously play an enormous role in his life, he always puts his family first.

TRIPPING POINT

A great story told by a new friend is more intoxicating than even the best Chianti Classico.

CHAPTER 23   THE CHARM OF ITALY'S BOOT

DESTINATION Osteria Le Logge, Siena

INSPIRATION Thanks to Colin and Sam Hanks' stellar recommendations, we have a night so full of love that I am nearly betrothed to a waiter named Walter.

• • • • • • • • • • • • • • • • • • • •

When I met Sam and Colin Hanks, they were fighting. More specifically, boxing—I pitted them against each other while running the Wii Lounge at Sundance and they laughed their way through it. Sam and Colin had sent me pages on what to do in Italy. They went there every summer with the entire Hanks clan. Knowing how happy and in love they are, I figured anything they suggested would have that Hanks family spirit and be good for the heart. As my parents and I settled into dinner at Osteria Le Logge in Sienna, recommended by both the Hanks and our vineyard host Andrea, I knew we were good.

Osteria Le Logge was simple—tiled floor, wooden chairs, and white table cloths. Sometimes it's the simple that satiates us. Recently I was at a "gratitude dinner" in Napa with Summit Series, a group that brings together entrepreneurs, and I felt a similar overwhelming and surprising appreciation for the food. Our "gratitude dinner" homework was to read Michael Jordan's "Love Letter to Basketball." If you haven't read it, go Google it immediately. Don't read on until you've done it, seriously.

That dinner filled me up for weeks. Michael Hebb, a self-proclaimed "architect for food," described our meal and insisted it was made with love. Farmer's market fruits and vegetables were chosen based on how ripe and "love-fit" they felt and then were paired accordingly. I swear I digested that meal better than any I'd had in years.

179

Angie, we stayed in a villa near Siena so our trips were around the Chianti region. Siena is an amazing city with so much to do – in some ways more enjoyable than Florence as it is more manageable. Great shopping, great food. You must go see the Duomo (cathedral) there – it is extraordinary! Also the museum of art. For dinner: Osteria Le Logge, Via del Porrione 33, off the northeast corner of the Campo – it's right near Loggia del Papa, which is on most maps. Make reservations 0577.48.013 and request seating downstairs in the old pharmacy. It's WAY nicer than the uneventful upstairs.

Life centers on the Piazza del Campo, the shell-shaped town square that is widely regarded as the most beautiful in Italy. For me, heaven is buying a Herald Tribune and a Guardian at Felterini, an outlet of a very good Italian chain on the main street, and sitting for an hour in the campo at dusk. We favor the bar called "Il Palio," for its – no lie, Harvey – superb mojitos with fresh mint. There are good Gelaterias on the square, the best being the one right on the main entrance that leads up to the Duomo; it has a tiny balcony on the Campo with two little benches.

The meal with Mom and Dad felt like it was built on the same premise. We savored the food and wine and each other's company, sighing with love and gratitude and discussing how we could best thank Andrea for the wonderful day we'd had at Geggiano. Next to us, a large, traditional Italian family tore through course after course. The dinner was special not so much because of anything that was said, but simply because we were so present. That must be why the Italians say *a tavola non s'invecchia*—at the table, no one grows old. Time stops.

After our long, love-filled Italian dinner, Mom and Dad announced they weren't ready for bed yet and decided we should go for one more drink. This was a rarity—maybe even a first!

Siena is built around a large, circular red-brick plaza, the Piazza del Campo, once a marketplace. Today the Piazza is lined with mom-and-pop restaurants and touristy shops, and the middle is a lively, open public square. It reminded me of Central Park, where I lay on the grass and watched the picnickers on many a summery Sunday during my six-month stint as a New Yorker. Piazzo del Campo is the night version, with crowds of people enjoying live music—dancing, lying in folded out chairs, staring up at the night sky, playing with babies, and spooning gelato.

Mom and Dad walked ahead, hand in hand, as I followed behind, distracted by the sights and sounds. We found Il Palio, where Sam had recommended the mojitos, and settled into a table where the sounds of jazz provided the first buzz. We sat as close as we could get. Our mojitos arrived and the mint and lime were refreshing, giving kick to the jazz beats.

Normally, Mom and Dad barely last past midnight, but as 2 a.m. passed, they insisted they weren't even tired. We had been swept into some magic, first by Andreas in the vineyard, and now in the piazza. The musicians must've been flown in from around the world—they were so good. The mojitos had to have been mixed by the top mixologist in Europe. We were convinced that all the gelatos and restaurants and people in the town had come to this shell-shaped square at night to create the perfect circumstances to recognize and celebrate the beauty of living.

Guy Banicki loved that he got to stay up late drinking with his wife—this was a novelty—and so he encouraged our waiter, Walter, to keep the mojitos coming. Every time I glanced over at Dad, he was leaning back in his chair, laughing and sipping his drink. Growing up, Dad was an active role model in our community—to kids at school, to parents trying to do the right thing, to teachers who strived to be examples. Dad enjoyed life and being that mentor more than I probably even knew, but man, it was nice to see him loosen up as we both aged. No forehead scrunching, no fingers tapping nervously—just laughing and snapping his fingers to the jazz, and reaching out to touch his wife's knee and smiling the smile that said, "Our life is good. I am happy by your side right here, right now in this moment." I got a squeeze on my shoulder and I instinctively reacted like a teenager, shrugging and smiling while rolling my eyes, but deep down I knew Dad was touching me to remind me to remember those moments.

I was surrounded by love— the love of my parents, the memories of love between Colin and Sam, and a city that loved. My parents told me that night that they're more in love than

SIENA'S 17 WARDS

BEFORE VISITING, DO TAKE THE TIME TO READ A BIT ABOUT SIENA'S HISTORY, AND ITS UNIQUE CITY STRUCTURE: IT IS DIVIDED INTO 17 WARDS, KNOWN AS CONTRADAS, WHICH SERVE THE SOCIAL HUBS, REPOSITORIES OF LOCAL HISTORY, MINI-CITY GOVERNMENTS, AND MOST IMPORTANTLY, THE PARTICIPANTS IN THE PALIO RACE TWICE A YEAR. WHEN YOU WALK AROUND, YOU'LL LEARN TO IDENTIFY WHICH CONTRADA YOU ARE IN BY LITTLE CERAMIC SHIELDS BUILT INTO THE CORNERS OF BUILDINGS. FOR SIENESE, THEIR FIRST ALLEGIANCE IS TO THEIR CONTRADA, THEN TO SIENA, WITH ITALY RUNNING A DISTANT THIRD. SIENA IS A COMPLETELY INTACT MEDIEVAL CITY THAT CLOSED ITS CENTER TO TRAFFIC IN THE 1960S. ALSO, UNLIKE FLORENCE, IT ISN'T PRIMARILY ABOUT TOURISM. IT IS HISTORICALLY A BANKING CENTER, HOME TO THE OLDEST BANK IN ITALY, AND IT HAS SEVERAL UNIVERSITIES. ALL THIS ADDS A FANTASTIC ENERGY TO WHAT SHOULD BE A PROVINCIAL CITY. —SAM HANKS they've ever been, a declaration that made me both embarrassed and content. The question of whether I, too, should be participating in this love, with a partner of my own, hung very gently in the air.

But not for long: Italy's finest was quickly on the job of romancing Angie. Our waiter, Walter, announced that we could marry and move to his beautiful homeland of Sicily, where together we should start a shoe business. Yes, a shoe business.

My father was only too happy to playfully egg him on.

"You know, Angie really does have good business sense."

Thanks, Dad.

BIO»

COLIN AND SAM HANKS

Sam and Colin Hanks, so in love, have become parents since my trip. They were married in 2010 and now they are a family with Olivia. Since their Italy dossier, they have given me the best travel advice for destinations all over the world, from Greece to India. Colin was raised in a showbiz family—Tom Hanks is his father, which is pretty obvious when you see Colin—and has become a talented TV and film actor in his own right. His biggest role to date was in the good-natured comedy "Orange County," but you'll also find him in some of today's best TV shows, including "Dexter" and "Mad Men."

▰ TRIPPING POINT ▰

A tavola non s'invecchia. At the dinner table, time stops.

CHAPTER 24 TOUCHDOWN AT THE VATICAN

DESTINATION Vatican City, Rome

INSPIRATION Friend of Patriots quarterback Tom Brady, Will McDonough, scores me the Vatican tour reserved for sports stars, U.S. presidents, and now, Angie Banicki.

● ● ● ● ● ● ● ● ● ● ● ● ● ● ● ● ● ● ●

As I approached the fountain in St. Peter's Square for my "Tom Brady Tour of the Vatican," I scolded myself for being late once again. My tour guide Davide was the Secretary to the Chancellor at the Vatican, and even though I'm still not sure what exactly that means, it sounded important enough that I should be on time. His VIP status was later confirmed when I learned that he lives next door to the Pope! And while I'm not religious myself, I was very aware that I was going to be touring the less-seen corners of a place that two-fifths of the world, including my parents, considers most sacred.

Walking up to Davide, his eyes told me he was waiting for me. I was ready with a rush of apologies for being a few minutes tardy. He stopped me right away, holding up his hand. He had a look that was both serious and gentle, with the methodical physicality that comes with being in the army.

"Angie, nice to meet you. Do you have a shawl or sweater?"

Oops.

Well, at least Jenna Bush forgot, too, according to Davide. She had made the same mistake of arriving with uncovered shoulders the day before. A few minutes later I wrapped a new yellow pashmina, purchased in a gift shop nearby, around my shoulders. I was now wearing white and yellow, not coincidentally the colors of the Vatican flag. It quickly became very real to me that the Holy See operated on a com-

185

pletely different set of very ancient rules.

What stuck out for me most on my tour was that I wasn't the only one who seemed a little bit trapped by the collision of tradition and modernity here at Rome's center. Because Davide was part of the Guardia Svizzera, the famous Swiss Guard charged with protecting the Pope and his city, the most special part of my tour was getting to meet and interact with some of the young guards.

Impossible to miss in their colorful costumes, the Swiss Guard has been protecting the Pope since 1506. Today's recruits are between 19 and 30 years of age and at least 174 cm (5'8") tall. They have to have been in the Swiss Army, and maybe most importantly, they need a note from their local priest saying that they're "Roman Catholic faithfuls" and "of a good moral ethical background." They commit to serving for two years, attending Mass once a week, and living in a barracks in Vatican City. Their rooms have TVs and their meals are all cooked by Polish nuns—"Good Swiss Italian food," according to one guard. When they're done, 95 percent return to Switzerland where the reputation of the Swiss Guard generally scores them a great job. Essentially, despite their circus attire, they're Switzerland's most eligible bachelors.

I trailed behind Davide as he marched in all his serious authority up to the gates these young men guarded. With barely an intro, Davide placed me between the two colorful guards who smiled nervously at me. Davide took my camera and said, "The best photo will be of you and the

FROM **Will McDonough**
TO **Angie Banicki**
subject **30Before30**

Angie, do you want the special tour we took with Tom Brady at the Vatican? They do it for US Presidents.
-Will

HISTORY OF THE SWISS GUARD UNIFORM

IT IS MAINLY THANKS TO COMMANDANT JULES REPOND (1910-1921), WHO WAS GIFTED WITH AN EXCEPTIONALLY FINE TASTE FOR COLORS AND SHAPES, THAT THE SWISS GUARDS WEAR SUCH FINE DRESS TODAY. AFTER MUCH STUDY AND RESEARCH AND DRAWING INSPIRATION FROM RAFFAELLO'S FRESCOES, HE ABOLISHED ALL TYPES OF HATS AND INTRODUCED THE SIMPLE BERET WORN TODAY, WHICH BEARS THE SOLDIER'S GRADE. THE COLORS WHICH MAKE THE UNIFORM SO ATTRACTIVE ARE THE TRADITIONAL MEDICI BLUE, RED, AND YELLOW, SET OFF NICELY BY THE WHITE OF THE COLLAR AND GLOVES. THE BLUE AND YELLOW BANDS GIVE A SENSE OF LIGHTNESS AS THEY MOVE OVER THE RED DOUBLET AND BREECHES. IT IS COMMONLY THOUGHT THAT THE UNIFORM WAS DESIGNED BY MICHELANGELO, BUT IT WOULD SEEM RATHER THAT HE HAD NOTHING TO DO WITH IT.
—FROM THE OFFICIAL WEB SITE OF THE VATICAN

guards under this arch." Yes, sir.

After chatting with the guards, who were shy with their broken English, I told Davide they reminded me of what I wore when I was the court jester in our high school madrigal. I didn't say it, but they also reminded me of my more famous costume: Northwestern's Willie the Wildcat. Laugh if you want to, but try putting on a mascot costume and tell me you don't have the time of your life. It's actually kind of like traveling—inside that big costume, you can be whoever you want to be.

I made Davide give me the history on the colorful guard costumes and I teased that he should wear one as well. Then the guards spoke in Italian to Davide and I asked him what they talked about. He said they rarely get to talk to girls and were happy they got to be in your picture. He also said they asked why he got to tour me, and not them.

"You made their day, Angie!"

"They made my day, Davide!"

Three months later I received a signed blessing from the Pope.

BIO ▶▶

WILL MCDONOUGH

I met Will, Tom Brady's advisor and friend, while doing the Playboy parties for the Kentucky Derby and the Superbowl. I'd always coordinate their tables and arrival with Will. He and Tom always showed up with a fun group in tow. I give Will most of the credit for that. He can bring the fun out of anyone and everyone. He's also one of those guys who's always working, but seems like he's never working. His relationship with the New England Patriots goes back to high school, when he moonlighted from his role as student body president to be an unpaid intern for the Patriots.

TRIPPING POINT

Outside your country, you're like a mascot at an away game.
Be yourself but respect the home turf you're on.

CHAPTER 25 TAKE A HIKE

DESTINATION Cinque Terre, Italy

INSPIRATION "Scrubs" star Sarah Chalke tells me to take a hike.

● ● ● ● ● ● ● ● ● ● ● ● ● ● ● ● ● ● ●

"ONLY IN A QUIET MIND IS ADEQUATE PERCEPTION OF THE WORLD."

—Hans Margolius

Rome is colossal and beautiful, but after leaving to visit Siena and Florence with my parents, I decided I might need to see more of Italy and the Italians. But was I really going to travel all the way up to Cinque Terre, more than five hours away? Sarah Chalke had recommended it. I'd always admired Sarah's big brain and even bigger heart, so I knew I should probably just do whatever she said. Also, Cinque Terre is known for its hike across five towns. I was named the Mayor of Runyan Canyon, Hollywood's most convenient hiking destination: Thank you, foursquare. I live, eat, and breathe for a good hike. Plus, I wanted to be near the calming influence of water, and the Cinque Terre path was through the cliffs above the beautiful Ligurian Sea.

Decision made. Cinque Terre, here I come.

How the heck am I going to get there?

My friend AJ DiPersia told me to rent a car and explore. AJ's family was Italian—they knew the territory. Of course he could do that. I'm adventurous but not insane. I pictured myself veering onto the wrong side of the road or worse, getting lost at night.

I would not, could not, in a car.

When he was in Italy shooting "When in Rome," Dax Shepard rode around on a moped.

His email had said, "Rent a moped, it's the only way to go."

189

Dax is a racecar driver—for real. He came on a trip I did to the Audi racecourse in Sonoma and he was practically teaching the racecar drivers. Basically a pro. My head says no moped.

I would not, could not, in a moped.

Mom and Dad fixed that. They sent me on the same train they took.

A train! A train! Would you, could you, on a train?

Yes, the ham I am will go there on a train.

As I set off by rail, I felt dueling personalities emerging from within. One part of me was raring to be on my own again, independent and charging through the Ligurian hills. The other part was feeling five years old and missing my parents and everyone else. I arrived in Montteroso, the first town of the five, as night fell. I looked around at my small, cold, cheap hotel room and decided to leave for a short walk in the town. The moon glistened on the water and I watched families eating at all the quaint outdoor restaurants, enjoying the view.

Cinque Terre was the first place where I didn't have a person to meet—no one to check in and make plans with. Just me. No wonder I felt lonely. Normally, I would avoid these kinds of feelings by throwing myself into work or social life, which were often one and the same. On the trip I was trying to embrace these emotions, live them through and suck some wisdom out of the experience.

Not long ago, my dad was admitted to the hospital with a blood clot, and the doctor told him he'd have to stay for the weekend. My father jumped out of the bed and, in his hospital gown and bare feet, started running in place to show the doctor how fit he was to go home immediately. That struck me as exactly how I had been handling my loneliness, and really any negative emotion—finding ways to run in place, or just literally run, rather than to face them.

That night, back in my bed, I drifted off to sleep still pondering these issues, and wondering whether the trip was really changing me.

When I awoke, BOOM: Runner Angie was back, excited to begin

the hike. I stopped in the hotel lobby for a quick breakfast. As I ate my croissant, I imagined my parents sitting with me, wildly excited as they would be about the availability of free food. The thought highlighted the upside of being alone and in control, even if the loneliness of the night before hadn't entirely left me.

I walked along the water in the direction of the hike's start. From the edge of town to the grassy land, I didn't see a single person until I arrived at the "tollbooth" for hikers, where I paid the attendant the small fee for my Cinque Terre admission ticket and eagerly set off.

The Cinque Terre hike goes something like this:

Monterosso–Vernazza: 2 miles

Vernazza–Corniglia: 1.5 miles

Corniglia–Manarolo: 1 mile

Manarolo–Riomaggiore: ½ mile

Everyone I spoke to said that I should either train there and hike back, or hike to the end and then train back. But with the sun on my back, the breeze blowing at me, and the beauty surrounding me, why would I not want to soak in all of it for as long as I could? I was set on powering through to make it there and back in one trip.

I catapulted along the trail, and as usual when I run, quickly found myself lost in thoughts—emotional ones, still working through the loneliness—and highly concentrated on moving my body through space. Weirdly, moving through space just allowed me to retreat further into myself. And then I turned a corner and SLAM—I hit the cliff. I tripped, almost stumbled, then caught myself and gasped. It was like a message from the universe: "Pay attention! Look outward! Get out of your head!"

After covering the half-mile over rocky ground, under trees, over branches and rocks, I had suddenly run out of path and was overlooking the most beautiful sublime vision I had ever seen. If you've ever run along the ocean, you know the sensory high. This was that, yet…more.

I had miles to go but I decided to let go, for a few minutes, of my powering-through plan. I stopped and breathed in air that seemed like nothing my senses had ever smelt, felt, or seen. I was dumbfounded and so full of the sensation that for the first time since I had left Rome, had no sense whatsoever of feeling alone. I felt full and awake and alive, emotions released and flying, buoyed also by the brilliant blue sea.

I took another deep breath and tried to memorize the feeling for later. Then I prepared to move on. Plans are plans, and I still wanted to make it back to Monterosso for dinner at Sarah's recommendation, CIAK. A sign told me I had reached Vernazza, so I still had four more towns and back to go. I pushed play on my iPod and shot ahead.

The second city began as a half run, half walk. Weaving along the cliff and inside the path, I was now running, but not running away. I was savoring my surroundings, feeling comfortable and energized in my skin, at peace in my head. Somewhere between towns two and four, I ran past a group of hikers who all smiled at me—the kind of smile that says, "Are you out of your mind?"

I must have been a sight in my neon pink shorts and army-green backpack, with my BlackBerry in my sweaty hand. The youngest and smallest of the group caught my eye and pulled a grin out of me as his big eyes stared and he smiled and pointed. He began clapping his hands, cheering me on as I ran past. I had a fan club of one! The genuine, irrepressible energy he exuded put an extra pep in my step, and I thought, this little guy just pushed me harder. He reminded me there's always someone looking out.

I continued my run and soon forgot about the family as the sun charged me forward. I passed other hikers along the way—an older couple, a few college-age kids, and locals out for the view. Every smile and hello pushed me on. I could keep running forever.

I had to force myself to stop for a bite. I hate eating when I'm not hungry, and in my run zone, I lose my appetite. But at town four on

CINQUE TERRE

THE CINQUE TERRE IS ONE OF THE MOST UN-CONTAMINATED AREAS IN THE MEDITERRANEAN SEA. FIVE MILES OF ROCKY COAST BETWEEN TWO PROMONTORIES, FIVE SMALL TOWNS CASTLED UP ON STONE SPURS ALONG MINUS-CULE CREEKS. FOR THEIR HISTORY AND THEIR POSITION, THE CINQUE TERRE HAS NOT SUF-FERED A MASSIVE EXPAN-SION. THE CINQUE TERRE OFFERS BEAUTIFUL FOOTPATHS WITH BREATH TAKING VIEWS, CHURCH-ES, ORATORIES AND OLD CASTLES, DIVING, FOOD AND WINES OF THE FIN-EST QUALITY. RIOMAG-GIORE, CORNIGLIA, MANAROLA, VERNAZZA, AND MONTEROSSO ARE THE FIVE VILLAGES THAT FORM THE CINQUE TERRE, SUSPENDED BETWEEN SEA AND LAND ON SHEER CLIFFS UPON THE BEAUTIFUL SEA.

the Cinque Terre trail, I ran off the path anyway, knowing I would need to rejuvenate if I wanted to finish the journey there and back, and wanting to recreate the moment sent to me by my friend Mike Appel—his perfect sandwich. The town was one outdoor café after another, intermingled with mini-markets. The cobblestone streets of Manarolo were laden with tourists and locals lunching and drinking wine. I snuck in peeks, but as Mike had directed, I was on a mission for fresh mozzarella, pesto, Italian bread, and ripe tomatoes.

It didn't take long before I found what seemed to be the perfect little mom-and-pop grocery shop. Inside, the owner chatted with a woman shopper. I stood patiently waiting, but he didn't acknowledge me at all, this sweaty mess of a girl milling about his store. Finally I interrupted, asking for help finding pesto and explaining that I was on a mission to buy four specific items. He blinked at me, annoyed that I had interrupted him, and went back to his conversation. I just smiled and shrugged and set off to look on my own.

193

FROM   Sarah Louise
TO   Angie Banicki
subject **30Before30**

What a frikkin amazing trip. I'm so jealous!!

So, one of my fave places I've visited ever is cinque terre in italy, i know its not on your agenda, but im throwin it out there cause i think you'll love it. It's five little villages built into the side of the coast (I think probably few hrs. drive from Rome?? maybe 5? maybe train?) but gorgeous. You can hike through the vineyards in the side of the cliff form village to village, you can stay at all of them, but i recommend staying at the first bigger one, Monterosso, and eat at CIAK, one of best restaurants ive ever been to, hot sizzling platters of crab gnocchi and red wine and yummy!!!!!

And in Amsterdam you have to go to the Anne frank house, so moving, so devastating, but go.

Good luck, have the best time

xoox

Sarah

FROM   Mike Appel
TO   Angie Banicki
subject **No Subject**

Go hike in Cinque Terre and stop at one of the fishing villages there. Go to a little market and grab fresh pesto, fresh bread, tomatoes and fresh buffalo mozzarella and have a picnic on the pier.

When I had found everything and went to check out, I turned to the woman he had been talking to, who seemed a lot friendlier, and asked her to take a picture of me with my sandwich supplies.

She laughed, "Why do you want a picture in this store?"

"Well…I have to send my friend Mike proof that I am carrying out his favorite travel moment."

I started explaining the story of my sandwich, the trip, all the moments I had collected. The woman was delighted, and suddenly the shop owner who had ignored me so completely had a total reversal. He too now wanted to hear about how his shop had become a destination for my journey—so much so that he butted into our conversation and offered to take the picture for me.

When I finished explaining my mission, he said, "You are magic. I like this idea."

It was cute—he wanted to make my and Mike's moment his, too.

I went outside to find a spot to eat on the cliff that looked out on the water. With no utensils, no napkins, just a paper bag and my bare hands, I slathered on the mozzarella, broke the bread, tore apart the juicy tomatoes and poured on the pesto. I felt barbaric but enjoyed it. It all looked like a bloody mess held between grimy hands, but once I tasted the freshness of all real ingredients, it was impossible to stop. Halfway through, I looked up to see a cute couple who had also found my spot on the stony cliff and wondered for a second if they would be revolted. But no, they were so in love they barely saw me, and I grinned, pesto and tomato juice dripping down my chin. You might think they made me feel lonely, this picture-perfect couple sharing a picture-perfect view, but not at all. I felt like where I was, and who I was—a mysterious stranger enjoying the sun and the view and a sandwich—was perfect for me. After I had cleaned myself up, I took a picture of them together, let myself share the moment with them, and then moved on.

Soon, I made it to the end of town five and felt accomplished. I looked onward and back and did what I do at Runyon Canyon in LA—I touched the signpost, flip turned, and kept on running.

At that point, the sun was really beating down and I felt a little drained. I downshifted to a walk, enjoying the challenge. As I moved along, my mind started walking through my journey to date—Italy, my parents, Paris, the dandy, the drinks… all the people I'd met and all the stories were like an unusually delicious energy drink pushing me forward. Every time I turned over another memory, another surge of energy burst through, and I'd find myself back to running. I continued this way back—run, walk, run, talk to myself—sometimes aloud.

Somewhere between towns four and three, I almost ran smack back into that same family from the morning run. As I slowed down to jog past them, the little boy yelled, "Look, Dad. It's that same runner girl."

This time I laughed out loud, just as he said, "What is she doing? How far did she go?"

Appreciating the break, I looked back and turned to walk toward the little guy, who was staring so incredulously at me that I laughed even more.

"I haven't been running this whole time! I walked some too!"

"Are you here alone? Why are you running that much?" he asked me, full of questions now that he had my attention.

The young parents and two other women traveling with them who I later learned were sisters, and aunt were not much older than me, and gorgeous, possessed of Northern European beauty, emanating kindness. All I saw were big smiles with gorgeous white teeth and muscular legs—legs that didn't look like they'd been sitting at desks all year long.

I laughed. "I am alone."

I am alone.

"We didn't mean to bother you or stop your run," the wife said with sincere concern.

"Come walk with us!" The little boy blurted.

"Jacko needs to practice his English and he's smitten with you," the father added with a smile.

This family of characters put me immediately at ease, and I decided that "lonely" had been properly explored, recognized, and appreciated—for the moment. I'd join them, curious about the happy group and excited to share part of Cinque Terre with someone.

We all set off, and Little Jacko came to tug on my shirt with more and more questions.

"How old are you? Are you married?"

I learned as we hiked along that he was actually quite small for his age. I had put him at 7, but actually he was 12, which his father, Leon, later informed me made it hard for him to make friends. Leon also told me it was great having me around because it forced Jacko's English. I took turns hiking alongside different members of the group, but the little guy was definitely my favorite. They apologized a few times for holding me back, but I assured them I was in need of family time and a break.

"Well then, look at the sun going down," Leon pointed. "Will you come drink wine at sunset with us in Vernazza?"

"Ahh, tempting, but I have to make it back for dinner at CIAK!"

"You can come for a little bit!!!!" How was I going to say no to the adorable Jacko?

"I still cannot believe you are alone!" Leon repeated. He was handsome and chiseled and seemed to be the caretaker of the group. But why wasn't he paying more attention to his beautiful wife? I almost felt uncomfortable with how friendly he was with me while she followed behind. She didn't seem bothered at all, though. Foreign thing? Open relationship? Oh boy.

Or maybe he was just taking care of his 12-year-old son's crush?

About halfway through city two, the truth came out.

"My brother is such a teaser," said the "wife."

"Ahhhhh. Yes, he is," I said of the attractive young father. They were brother and sister, not husband and wife, and his flirtation had been completely natural and normal. I sighed in relief, and then started dissecting a new question: Was I even interested in Leon?

Enough so that after things were clear, I agreed to have wine with the family. We stopped in town two and I reminded them I had to be back in Monterosso in time to shower and make it to CIAK.

We pulled up plastic outdoor chairs around a long table. We hydrated and agreed to a few bottles of wine. Leon joked about how lucky they were to convince the marathon hiker to join them, and I giggled. Like I was back on the first rocky outcropping of the hike, I let myself get lost in the moment, laughing and flirting, completely at ease. Leon continued to top off my wine and I felt my head floating. Jacko was looking around in my backpack and I teased him, trying on his glasses. The sisters were telling me about college in the Netherlands. The instant camaraderie was as pleasant as the now-cooling air.

I felt the moment arrive when I knew I had to either stay with this family or get on the train to make it in time to CIAK. I imagined the scenario if I stayed: Me and my fan club, which had doubled its membership now to two (Jacko and Leon), would stay until the bottles were empty and the sun dipped well below the horizon. Then we'd go to a bonfire. Maybe Leon and I would take a moonlit walk, exchange kisses, and laugh some more.

It sounded nice—but truthfully, not as nice as a sizzling plate of crab gnocchi and the pleasure of getting to tell Sarah about it when I got back. It felt incredible to realize that as much as I was glad for a break from my job, I still missed the people that it brought me in touch with— the part that really mattered.

"It's 9 p.m. I have to get back to CIAK!" I announced with determination. I chose alone.

The decision was made, and though Leon made more than one attempt to lure me to the bonfire they had planned, they realized soon that I was really on my way. I knew what I wanted and it felt good to act on it.

Later at CIAK, inhaling bites of the incredible gnocchi, tired legs dangling from my chair, I felt for one of the first times in my life that I was truly happy having a moment in which I was my own and only fan club.

Cinque Terre was the place where I learned to be totally alone without being lonely.

BIO ►►

SARAH CHALKE

Sarah plays Dr. Eliot Reid on "Scrubs." In real life, she's always funny without being mean and raunchy—she's smart and quick, and that's all she needs. She's now a loving mother who at one point sent my entire office milk and cookies as a thank-you for taking her on one of our Vegas trips. My favorite memory, though, is dancing with Sarah on the dingy dance floor of the "SNL" after-after party one late night in New York—not so uncommon for me but it was special because of Sarah!

TRIPPING POINT

Don't power your way through loneliness. Embrace it, and know when to let others in.

QUICK HITS | ROME

FRED WILLARD | ACTOR, "BEST IN SHOW"

...Rome: The most wonderful city in the world. Romantic, friendly, and breathtaking. As you taxi to your hotel you will pass sites you've read about your entire life,"Oh, there's the seven hills! Oh, there's the circus maximus where Ben Hur raced his chariot! Oh, there's the colosseum!" **Once you have seen the colosseum by day or in the moonlight you will never forget it. It stands as a testament to man's ability to create beauty.** You will sigh with wonder at the immenseness of it...

• •

DAVID BUGLIARI | AGENT, CAA

...try to speak some Italian phrases...it's a sign of respect that American's rarely do.....chances are, they speak English...but **say a few words or questions in Italian...it gets you some street cred...**

• •

JESSE LUTZ | CAMERON DIAZ'S ASSISTANT

...There is an amazing paper shop right next to the Pantheon, which is a very cool thing to see, and if you like paper, beautiful photo albums, etc. There is also a famous gelateria on the walk there....you can't miss, very large and famous. There is also the well known Il Papiro by the Trevi fountain...**There is a gelateria at every corner..I recommend at least one a day**. Il Bacio, or the kiss is a chocolate hazelnut you should have....there's one by the pantheon that is insanely delish!...The view from Giancolo Hill is unbelievable, a nice walk, and there is a merry go round at the top....breathtaking, panoramic view of the city...

• •

EMMY ROSSUM | "PHANTOM OF THE OPERA", "SHAMELESS"
...ROME -- EAT ALOT. you can't have a bad meal wherever you go or however much you spend. the regular panini shops are great, get everything with mozzerella, **all the men are gorgeous, even the panini maker boys**...

• •

ERICA BRAY | TRAVELZOO
...Beautiful cobblestone streets. If you plan to do walking (and you SHOULD—just be careful of the crazydrivers), **bring comfortable shoes. Just don't be surprised to see the Italian women strutting around in stilletos**... (I have no clue how they do it.)

RICK FOX | ACTOR

…We landed in Rome the night of the finals of the world cup Italy versus France. We checked into the Hotel at Spanish Steps then walked to Circus Maximus where we watched the final 20 minutes of the world cup with 300,000 italians… the italian team won and we stormed the streets of rome chanting the white strips song with the celebrating fans…**we swam in the Trevi Fountain with hundreds of italians and walked the streets of Rome till the sun came up kissing random Italian girls who were drunk and happy to be World Cup Champions**… The next day we rented scooters and followed behind the team bus that rode through town on their return to Rome….Oh yeah took a tour of the Vatican, Coliseum, and other Roman sights but it all paled in comparison to swimming in the Trevi fountain…

• •

BRYAN GREENBERG | ACTOR, "HOW TO MAKE IT IN AMERICA"

…Ask a tour guide or someone from your hotel to show you **the view from the Key Hole.** Not everyone knows about it but it's worth it…

• •

JASON REITMAN | DIRECTOR, "JUNO", "UP IN THE AIR"

…If you don't stop for gelato in Rome at "San Crespino" near the Trevi Fountain, you're out of your fucking gourd. **Order the pear gelato…**

• •

IAN ZIERING | ACTOR, "90210"

…There's a small restaurant in the Trastevere area of Rome called "Popi Popi." It's a tad nicer then a pizza place but **what sets it apart is the fact that the outside seating area is in the courtyard of a beautiful church**. I recall going there and being awed by the magnificence of it. I would go just before it got dark and quite often musicians would be there playing violins and flutes. Very special place…

• •

BEN LYONS | CORRESPONDENT, "EXTRA"

…Walk the Spanish steps late at night. I did my one and only night in Rome and it was breathtaking. During the day, it's a tourist nightmare, but late at night, when its completely empty, you get the most amazing feeling…

• •

JON LOVITZ | SATURDAY NIGHT LIVE

…I haven't been to Europe since 1978. But my advice is to go to Venice. It is amazing, like Disneyland, surreal. All the taxis are boats. On the other hand, if you hate water, skip it. Rome…I'd go to the Spanish steps…it's these old steps, but as I recall, **you can see all the ruins from there…**

QUICK HITS | ROME

MILO VENTIMIGLIA | ACTOR, "HEROES"

…The sunset on the hill from the Piazza d'Michelangelo in Florence is beautiful. I took a bunch of pictures, but none do justice to how I remember it, **a very pink sky, like a grapefruit.** We ate at a little restaurant with no sign called COCO Lezzano, family owned, and we got there so late the family was just sitting down for their meal too…

• •

COLIN HANKS | ACTOR

…Go to the Museum of Natural History known as "La Specola." Beyond the most extensive collection of flea-bitten taxidermy on the planet, it features room upon room of anatomically perfect wax figures that were created in the early 18th century as teaching tool for medical students. **It's like a Vincent Price movie come to life**, and somehow manages to be beautiful, melancholic, scary and perverse at the same time…

• •

CHRISTIAN OLIVER | ACTOR

…When in Rome **EAT DRIVE LOVE**… and always wear a helmet!…

• •

KEISHA AND FOREST WHITAKER

…We love ROME. We had a great time when we spent a romantic Valentines Day there in '07. We had a fantastic dinner and then threw coins in the Trevi fountain **(don't forget to make a wish)**…and walked outside the Colosseum….And you must have a photo on the Spanish Steps!!…

• •

Amsterdam

CHAPTER 26 ON THE TRAIN GANG

DESTINATION Eurorail's Employees Only Area

INSPIRATION Meat Loaf's wife Deborah tells me she and Meat (yes, she calls him Meat) enjoyed seeing Europe via train. Encouraged, I decide to train it from Rome to Amsterdam, via Venice: 14+ hours.

• • • • • • • • • • • • • • • • • • •

If the Eurostar was good enough for Meat Loaf, it was good enough for me—plus I couldn't afford the expensive plane ticket to go from Rome to Amsterdam for the final leg of my trip. After a jumble of a time getting to the train station and a rumble of one finding the right train to get myself to Amsterdam, I stepped into the car with the feeling another adventure was waiting to happen.

I had barely settled into my seat on the first leg, from Rome to Venice, before I started feeling claustrophobic and antsy. I decided to go in search of snacks. Finding the old '50s-looking train bar, I stood in front of the bar, staring dazedly at the menu for far too long. After finally realizing there was nothing for vegetarians, I settled in to try to write.

My thoughts raced along with the train, but wouldn't come out of my fingers onto the laptop. I'd come so far in the last 24 days. The real world was speeding by, just the way it looked through the train window, and I was just floating, lost in thought. Until I felt eyes looming, and out of the corner of my eye saw that a man in a uniform was approaching. I turned the music up on my headphones and tried to type anything to avoid having to speak to this Trainman in his busting-at-the-seams olive uniform and disheveled hair that he kept smoothing down over his sweaty brow.

He walked up and stopped. I went with the half pull of a head-

Last summer Meat had a week off from tour and I booked us on the Eurostar train. Meat was not feeling up to par at the time but we did manage to get in a few sight-seeing trips before we had to leave. Personally, I love Paris. I really enjoyed the Chateau de Versailles, home of Louis XIV, XV, and XVI. Marie Antoinette also had her own home on the grounds. When I walked through her home I envisioned Marie herself walking through the same halls.

phone. In very broken English he stuttered, "You write? Want privacy? I have place?"

I wasn't about to go anywhere with this strange man, and I definitely didn't want to know what he had in his private place. This had "American girl murdered and shoved into a suitcase" written all over it. I must have scared him with my look because he stepped back and peered shyly under his sweaty brow after his question. I relaxed a little.

"I'm fine. Thank you," I said politely.

In broken style again: "It will fill up." He pointed around. "I have place in back. Other workers there too." He wasn't giving up.

The bartender, who had apparently been watching our exchange, piped up.

"He's harmless and if he takes you in back, you'll have your own space. They aren't supposed to bring people there."

"Luca." The trainman stretched out his hand to shake mine and I looked at him more carefully. The sweaty, unkempt appearance that at first said serial killer now looked more like Super Mario, from the Nintendo game I played as a kid.

I shrugged and gave in. Why not?

"I'm Angie!" I stretched out my hand out to shake his.

His face broke into a huge grin. Before I could change my mind, he volunteered to get my bag—and walked back to my train car to get it.

Luca beeped me past the commoners and into the Mushroom Kingdom—actually, the employee break room. He cleared the first big booth and spoke Italian to his coworkers, informing them that I'd be working in this corner booth, and needed privacy.

Before I could sit down, he was back offering me water and Diet Coke. "Eat? Food?" The exchange reminded me for some reason of the time that Dustin Hoffman liked the hors d'oeuvres so much at our BlackBerry event that he disappeared—and when we finally found him it was back in the kitchen where he'd gone to congratulate the chef.

I could see Luca appreciated food too. He told me the train's new chef was his friend, and later brought the young woman out to meet me. I tried to tell him I wasn't hungry. Not stopping Luca—he was full steam ahead with the snacks, coming at me every 15 minutes. And yet he was totally respectful of my being in "work mode," quietly dropping items on my table without making conversation.

After a few hours, I was feeling pretty comfortable in the employee car. One of Luca's coworkers finally disregarded his command that I was not to be bothered and came over to chat. I showed him pictures from my trip and we talked about Italy.

"Luca doesn't speak great English but he is a good man. He likes you."

He also told me that Luca was close to 40 and lived with his mother.

Slowly, other workers, mostly male, were joining our conversation. I was intrigued by their lifestyle—what was it like to work the rails?

"Where is your home base? Do you travel together all the time?" I asked. They took turns sharing and answering my questions.

BIO

MEAT LOAF

Ever wonder why Meat Loaf, whose album "Bat Out of Hell" is one of the best selling of all time, is called Meat Loaf? He's put out different stories over the years but recently told ESPN. com that Marvin Lee Aday was called "Meat" his entire life, but then when he was 13 his football coach in Texas added the "Loaf." Besides the fact that even his wife calls him "Meat," I love that ML is still rockin' out at 65.

Before long, a group of workers had packed into my little corner. One who must have had a weekend job drawing cartoon portraits on Montmarte drew a picture of Luca with a bubble saying, "I like Angie." We all laughed, and I could tell they all liked teasing Luca.

I finally closed the laptop and let myself enjoy this unusual peek behind the curtain. Conversation flowed. Luca knew English least but was content hanging around, laughing with the group. One of the workers brought out his camera for photos and I made him take photos with mine. It was playful and silly—score one for Super Mario.

TRIPPING POINT

Always follow the man (or woman) who offers to take you behind the curtain.

CHAPTER 27 THE COROZZA #7 BOXCAR

DESTINATION Amsterdam

INSPIRATION An email that wasn't part of the color-coded plan brings a shift of perspective.

● ● ● ● ● ● ● ● ● ● ● ● ● ● ● ● ● ● ●

It was 90 degrees and I was sweating balls as I switched trains in Venice, pushing my way through swarms of foreigners. Drenched in sweat, dress sticking to me—all I could think was thank God I had worn my bathing suit (at the time it just seemed right?). Somehow it all felt less gross with the swimsuit on.

I couldn't mask my discomfort, and it wasn't a pretty look. Worse, it had the potential to last 14 more hours, the length of the train ride. I walked the sweaty, smooshed walkway full of people, all yelling in different languages. I walked up to the door to my car and it opened before I could prepare myself. The car is the size of my closet. My face went from discomfort to horror.

"You've got to be kidding me." Oops, I said it aloud.

"Yeah...right?!" said a woman with long African dreads and a great big behind that spanned the width of the doorway. Dreads spoke English and wasn't a happy camper. Later I learned she was French.

"This is a joke, right?" Out loud again. Social grace, Angela!

The sixth spot in our cubbie of heat with a broken light was occupied by a 200-pound part-Samoa, part-Aski. Yes, I asked in the horror of the moment. The couple holding his leash completed the picture: They each outweighed their dog.

Dreads saw the dog and started shouting.

"Oh hell, no! That thing is not sleeping in here with me! Do you

> I know you're traveling, but wanted to fill you in. Nick H from spin passed away. He wasn't in spin class and they said he had a seizure. I'll keep you in the loop. This is what I know now. Sorry to have to tell you like this.

gotta ticket for that?? I demand to talk to a conductor."

"I'm not staying here," I chimed in.

The couple was sweet and quiet as can be as they told us that dogs are allowed on the train.

"Gestapo! I demand to speak to the Gestapo running this thing!" Dreads shouted. "I paid money for this seat and will not stay with this animal!"

Maybe it was the heat getting to me or the yelling, but suddenly I was on edge of erupting into uncontrolled laughter. The kind that comes out when it feels like it can't get much worse. And at just that moment, our final box-mate joined us: A six foot 7 inch bodybuilder who could eat the dog while bench-pressing all of us at once.

This was too much. As train officials arrived, I asked the pet owners if I could take a picture of their beautiful dog. Secretly, I was trying to photo the entire boxcar from Hell. The couple was nodding and so proud as their dog smiled for me. Holding back giggles, desperately needing air, I squeezed my way out.

In the hallway, my BlackBerry buzzed with an email.

My flailing emotions hit the ground hard. Nick was a friend of mine from college days—we'd worked together in Chicago at a bar and lounge called Sauce. He'd moved to LA too, and although we weren't as close now, he had just sent me a Facebook request a few days before. He had beautiful cheekbones, like a model, but back in our Sauce days was always ready to roll up his sleeves and have her back when a waitress needed help.

As tears welled and blended with my sweat, I found myself smiling, thinking about those days with Nick in Chicago.

Looking up, I wasn't alone. Dreads had followed me outside and didn't seem to notice my tears. She wasn't happy that I had bailed on talking to the train reps.

"Are you kidding me? Why were you smiling and taking pictures? You seemed as mad as me at first!"

I wiped away the tears, took a breath, sighed, and finally smiled at her.

"I was mad, but you know what, I decided to live it. I had to get a picture of that dog. Have you ever seen a dog that big? In a car so tiny?!"

She shook her head at me, but I saw her soften. Finally, she laughed too.

"If this is the worst thing that happens to us, we're doing all right," I added.

We headed back into the car, and now that Dreads and I had connected, it felt just a little bit bigger.

The bench-presser kindly took care of arranging our luggage.

And it got bigger still.

I sat. Petting the dog, I felt strangely comfortable to do what I might have run from anywhere else. (It helped that there was nowhere to go.) I let myself mourn an old friend.

TRIPPING POINT

Life can be a bitch—but sometimes all you've gotta do is find the funny. Train rides are a great way to ride it out.

CHAPTER 28 A STAR FROM A STAR

DESTINATION Amsterdam, The Netherlands

INSPIRATION David Arquette says that a tattoo from Hollywood Mark will expand my soul.

• • • • • • • • • • • • • • • • • • •

"SHOW ME A MAN WITH A TATTOO AND I'LL SHOW YOU A MAN WITH AN INTERESTING PAST."

—Jack London

Am I really going to get a tattoo from Hollywood Mark?

Tattoos are for rockers. Tattoos are for artsy hipsters. Tattoos give a girl an edge. Tattoos were always scary to me as a kid. But clowns were always scary to me too, and then I became one—my college's football mascot.

Never had I desired a tattoo—not even an inkling for the ink. But when someone like David is helping you "choose your own adventure," you want to choose everything he tells you. David is my secret—or not so secret—idol. He has success but it doesn't define him—he prefers to let his crazy costumes and karaoke stand out. He has a family and it has only changed him for the better. He spends his life giving but doesn't talk about it. He has friends who will do anything for him, and have. He is silly and forgetful and down to earth, but he is also a mature, successful adult.

Tattoos are for risk-takers. Tattoos are sexy. Tattoos give a girl confidence. Tattoos make you stronger. Tattoos lead us into the minds of those who have them. I'd like to have people wonder about my mind.

I was convinced…maybe. When I arrived in Europe, I was still teetering, so I did what most would do when contemplating a serious

215

Thank you for including me on this amazing journey. I wish for you a safe and soul-expanding trip... As for references in Amsterdam if you want to get a tattoo (yeah you asked me) a guy named Hollywood Mark has a place there and is a dear friend and hilarious person and perfect for a life changing soul-expanding experience. If you are interested in that please let me know and I'll get the address for you. In Amsterdam as far as Museums go Van Gogh - he was this wild character that cut his ear off... You may have heard of him. But really if no one else suggested it - it's a must although everyone walks around like it's the saddest place in the world and I feel quite the opposite. I'll try to shake up the old head to recall some not to be missed spots along your journey but for now it's just Amsterdam... Is that weird? Also maybe not as deep as you might think but you haven't met Hollywood Mark yet.

decision with long-term consequences. I stalled and avoided. Amsterdam was to have been my first city after London, but I went to Paris next instead. After that, Barcelona. Next, Italy just made more sense. And so Amsterdam became my last stop.

My tattoo dilemma had become like the pondering of a first kiss. You wait for the right moment, trying not to think about it, twisting your hair and making awkward conversation until you actually do the deed. Well, I flirted in every city and had built up this kiss so much that I wasn't even sure I could handle it. The more I thought about the moment actually happening, the scarier it became.

I should have known it was fated, though, when my tattoo artist's family adopted me before I had even arrived in the city. David had connected me to Mark, and then his wife, Sacha, emailed me, inviting me to stay with them.

Mark had met me outside the Schipol train station after my never-ending train ride from Rome. I'll be honest, the only things I connected with Amsterdam were pot, tattoos, and Anne Frank—a strange combination. I half-expected everyone to have a joint in hand, and for the Grateful Dead to be playing mysteriously in the background. Perhaps I wasn't altogether wrong as I watched herds of college kids with backpacks swarming out onto the streets and into the coffee shops. But the city itself felt more like a small country town than most of the places I had already been. And most importantly, it felt safe.

I felt even safer as I saw Mark walking over. He was very tatted up (expected) but also quite short (unexpected). His smile was comforting and kind.

"Did you make it okay? Were you waiting long? We are so excited to have you here!" He talked like David and some of David's childhood friends I knew—voice a little raspy, but lovingly concerned. Familiarity is a thing of beauty when you've been traveling and hearing only foreign languages. It was so nice to hear this sudden rush of home.

I chucked my suitcase into his Pinto and we hit the road for home. He was eager to show off his town, but family came first, which turned out to be one of Mark's defining qualities. "I wish we had more time now because I'd give you a tour by car," he told me. "We've got to pick up the cake for my daughter, Nicole. It's her birthday tomorrow and the bakery by the house closes soon. Sacha will not be happy if I don't go now!"

"I'm excited to meet your family! And I like exploring on my own on foot anyway."

The Pinto poked itself right into the lane. I loved the small-town feel of Amsterdam. No traffic, bustle, or hustle. Creeping over cobblestones and skimming the edge of the red-light district, I got just a sneak peek into the alleys with the peep shows and pot bars. I saw from a distance the famous canals.

As Mark and I continued the drive, he pointed out landmarks. "That way to Vondelpark and not far from there is the Van Gogh Museum."

BIO

DAVID ARQUETTE

I like to pretend that David Arquette's charm is a secret that no one is in on but me, but that's not really the truth. When I last saw him host a charity event, he got a lot of important people to do things they would never do for anybody else, ever. In my experience, convincing big celebrities is near impossible—they just get so many requests. (I did once convince Jack Nicholson to read *Walter the Farting Dog* at a charity event, but probably only because the Lakers had won the day I pitched.) People help David because they know David goes the distance. He once sat for two days in a plastic box on top of Madison Square Garden to raise hundreds of thousands of dollars for Feeding America. At the time he told DoSomething.org, "I'm a dork, I've always been a dork." And that's why I love him.

"Ah yes, my friend Bryan wants me to go ride a bike around Vondel—you can rent, right?" I was excited to share my research on his city.

"Wow, you really did get the full rundown!" Mark laughed.

We had reached more open land as we headed outside of the city toward Mark's house. Mark first moved from Hollywood to Amsterdam to become better at his craft and to gain perspective. His tattoo idol had invited him to come apprentice—I felt happy hearing he too had started a journey because someone had inspired him. He was only supposed to stay in Amsterdam for a year, but then he met Sacha. I thought about his story as he ran in to pick up the cakes.

"I still don't know how I got her," Mark explained as he jumped back in the pinto. "You'll see…she's gorgeous—a blonde from Sweden. I landed her, though. She wouldn't even give me the time of day when we met."

I laughed as we pulled up to the house. I was dying to meet this Scandinavian goddess. Mark was so easy going—laughing and making fun of himself as he told me about his determined pursuit of the woman who was to become his wife.

"Sacha turned me down time and time again. I kept asking her to play pool with me. I didn't care when she denied me. She laughed at my persistence, but I kind of think that's how I got her. I didn't give up."

We pulled up to their home and walked up to the second floor entrance of their condo-style house. It was far from spacious. In fact, it felt like the streets of Amsterdam—overflowing and full of heart. They were maxed out in every capacity, from children's toys to home supplies to love and affection. Mark and Sacha never let on for a second that I might be a bother, but I can only imagine the pressure of yet another guest, a.k.a. big child, crashing in their home.

We went straight for the kitchen to meet Sacha. I immediately saw how the couple was unique: She was at least a foot taller! She was quite the matriarch: cooking, cleaning, and mom-ing it with her children, arm around one and asking the birthday girl about school.

"Angie!! Welcome! We are so glad you are here!!"

She rolled her eyes at Mark when he opened the bakery box.

"Of course you forgot. Why did I even think you'd remember the second pie?"

She smiled at me as she teased him and I smiled back.

Grandma was in town visiting the family as well. That made me worry again about imposing on this busy family, but my fears were quickly dissolved when Mark's adorable mom, who is apparently half-deaf, yelled out, "How lucky are we to have this angel here sent to us by little David Arquette!?" I thought she was delirious or smoking the Amsterdam reefer, but Mark's wife looked at me with a smile and said with a hint of a laugh, "Yes, we are lucky."

It was a little bit like stepping into the Amsterdam edition of "Everybody Loves Raymond," and I loved it.

Of course, looming over it all was the issue of the tattoo. Over

THE NAUTICAL STAR

THE NAUTICAL STAR IS THE TRADITIONAL SAILOR'S TATTOO, SYMBOLIC OF LUCK, PROTECTION, AND OF FOLLOWING ONE'S TRUE PATH IN LIFE. THE STAR, RESEMBLING THE DISTINCTIVE COLOR PATTERN OF THE COMPASS ROSE FOUND ON MANY OLD NAUTICAL CHARTS, IS SAID TO REPRESENT THE NORTH STAR, THE KEYSTONE OF CELESTIAL NAVIGATION THAT COULD ALWAYS SHOW A SAILOR THE WAY HOME.

the next days, as I walked the streets of Amsterdam, I wondered if I got it, where I'd put it. I looked down at my feet. They had gotten me through some rough paths around Europe. From Hyde Park in the rain, to Gaudi Park on my most dehydrated-ever run, to trips (as in stumbles) all through Italy's ruins. I loved running in each country; it was my way of getting intimate quickly with each new city and its neighborhoods. Yes, definitely, my feet were a…shoe in. (Ha!)

Then I thought about what would look good, there on my foot. Something small but memorable. I knew it had to be a symbol of this trip. Could it be calligraphy? "30" wouldn't work. I couldn't look at 30 when I was 57. It couldn't be a name, or anything too long. I kept my eyes peeled, searching walls, paintings, and photos around Amsterdam for signs.

And then it appeared. I was standing on a bridge overlooking one of Amsterdam's famed canals when it came to me. Water rippling below, a summer breeze playing across my face, and there on my BlackBerry was the sign: a nautical star. It jumped out at me after pages and pages of images. I would be tattooed with the sailor's good luck symbol! It represented, I read, following one's true path in life. I got goose bumps. This was it. Later my mother told me that my grandfather, who had introduced me to the water, had gotten a tattoo when he was a sailor: a band around his wrist marked with a nautical star. The stars had aligned, literally.

The morning I was leaving Amsterdam, I went for my tattoo. I had waited until the absolute last moment, and it was time to pucker up. My palms were sweaty and my heart was beating out of my chest, but it was finally happening. My lips quivered as Mark drove me to his shop. He never pressured me and let me know every emotion was okay. Having spent the past days staying with Mark, his wife, and his three children, I could take comfort in the fact that my tattoo artist wasn't even the least little bit intimidating.

His tattoo parlor was bright and shiny and clean. Not like any tattoo parlor I had driven past in Hollywood with the neon signs, dark entrances, and eerie unknown behind the creepy lobby. This felt more like a 13-year-old skater's wet dream. There were cartoons and color all around. Mark brought over a size selection chart and we talked placement. I hadn't thought about that. So many details. How big? Where on my foot? All things to think about when getting a tat. This was a commitment, this kiss. It was about to make something permanent in my life.

"Mom and Dad aren't so keen on the tattoo," I explained to Mark as I asked for a slightly smaller version, pointing to the exact place on my foot.

Mark didn't seem surprised. "Kate Hudson got a star on her foot, too, and she had to call her mom first!" It was reassuring to hear that someone else also needed Mom's approval and even funnier that the Mom in question was Goldie Hawn.

The actual tattooing was pretty quick. I expected intense pain, but found it was much less painful than my pot brownie experience the night before. And I was a lot less scared too. I felt a tingle in my tummy as I watched Mark studiously buzz the beautiful star onto my foot. I felt myself smiling that goofy smile you couldn't wipe off if you tried—the kind you get when your lips finally touch in a kiss.

My time in Amsterdam was complete.

TRIPPING POINT

Tattoos make great souvenirs. Every time you see it, you're reminded to enjoy the journey.

CHAPTER 29 SAY NO TO SPACE CAKES

DESTINATION Betty's Café, Amsterdam

INSPIRATION Bryan Greenberg sends me to Vondelpark but a brownie fiend gets the best of me.

• • • • • • • • • • • • • • • • • • • •

This is the story of the $2,000 pot brownie.

Listen, I didn't wake up my first morning in Amsterdam planning to get high. I don't understand how people actually start their day like that, but I guess don't knock it 'til you've tried it. I woke up excited for a day of exploration. I took the bus into town and went straight for Vondelpark—Bryan Greenberg and the Meyers brothers' recommendation.

I'd barely begun my stroll when I got another email, from my brother's roommate, that changed my thinking:

"Go to this place Betty's. It's my favorite spot. Eat a pot brownie. Just sit there and relax. It's amazing people watching."

A pot brownie! At a café! Suddenly marijuana got a lot more attractive. Smoke alone I will not—not even a cigarette. But give me a brownie and I'll gobble it up.

So I went to Betty's. It all felt very PG, like an ice cream parlor in "Leave it to Beaver." Betty, an Asian 20-something, was all smiles and uncharacteristically friendly. She counseled me on flavors and highs. I had no idea what she was talking about, but one particular big brownie on the shelf seemed to be calling out to me.

Angie, eat me! Eaaaaat me!

I was still nervous about being high by myself and told Betty as much. She pushed her dark glasses up on her nose and looked me in the face. For some reason it was reassuring, as if she were really a

pharmacist. So I trusted her when she said, "Just eat half. It's totally
fine. It's not really gonna affect you—it won't hit you that hard."

I decided to sit down at the pot bar with my pharmacist, who would
keep an eye out for any suspicious behavior. I nibbled as Betty and I
chattered. I told her about Canaan, my brother's roommate, being the
reason I came, and she lit up behind the glasses and giggled, loving
that I'd been sent here all the way from LA. She pulled out two Betty's
lighters for Canaan and me.

We were now 10 to 20 minutes into my brownie. I'd had a quarter
and still felt nothing. Betty reassured me again, telling me I was fine to
have the other quarter. I obliged, then pocketed the rest and decided it
was time to go explore Amsterdam.

It was still light out, probably 4 p.m., with a breeze that reminded me of
a perfect day hiking in LA. I was feeling good, enjoying my walk along the
city's beautiful canals, when I decided to call an old friend and share the
moment.

Robbin, my friend from high school, was surprised to hear from
me—it had been a while since we'd spoken, and she knew I was over-
seas. We launched into excited conversation, and I realized I still wasn't

really feeling high.

"Robbin, I think I'm immune to pot. I'm not high, I mean, I think I'm not high. I'm happy but I don't feel anything." As I spoke, I broke out the other half and started nibbling off small pieces.

"The brownie is tasty though!"

Really, really tasty—suddenly, I couldn't stop, I wanted more sweets, more chocolate, more yummy goodness. And then the brownie was gone.

Robbin and I chatted until she reminded me how big my bill would be. Then I hung up and suddenly it hit me: "I think I'm really high."

Did I mention I was also completely lost?

Angie Panicki immediately took the scene. My inner monologue was something like this, as I called friend after friend in the states and got voicemail after voicemail: *I can't be alone and high. Oh my God, oh my God, I can't go back to my host's house. What am I gonna do? The kids, they have kids, the kids can't see me high. Will food help? I see a Greek restaurant. Nicole, my assistant, told me to go to Greece.*

Good enough. Please sober up. Food to soak up the brownie? You're not drunk; you're stoned! Then, once I had somehow gotten a table and ordered:
I can barely eat what this waiter has served me—it could be poisoned. It is poisoned. I don't know what to do. Stop looking at me. I must hang up.

They are listening...

And on and on and on.

I was pretty sure that everyone in the restaurant was watching me. The couple kitty corner to me was moving in slow motion—strange. It was as if they knew I was watching them watching me and were therefore being very calculating in their movements. I was on to it, but I also knew the conspiracy involved the entire restaurant. I watched as the man pretended to cut his gyro. I knew what he was thinking with that knife.

Wait: What did the man just slide across the table? Where is she going? Is her superwoman coat in the bathroom? Am I going to be kidnapped? Angie, stop being crazy. Talk quietly. Wait... I'm not talking.

It was almost dark. I wanted to be sober when I got back to Hollywood Mark's, who had been so kind to put me up, but I couldn't wait any longer—finding my way home in the dark would have been impossible. I was still lost, remember.

I started walking, and tried to get my friend Alana on the phone. Thank God she answered!

"Alana, I'm lost in Amsterdam and really high."

Laughter.

"This is not a joke. I'm serious."More laughs. "What happened, Angie?"

I pictured Alana, a casting director, sitting at her desk at Fox as I began my crazy nonstop monologue while simultaneously trying to get my bearings. She stayed with me—I had begged—while I searched for my bus stop, wrong turn after wrong turn, and then while I waited.

"Oh my God, everyone's watching me. They are laughing at me…. No, I'm at the bus stop—this is not funny; stop laughing." She couldn't stop laughing. I was just glad to have a friendly, familiar voice in my ear.

"Angie, just do me a favor right now. Take a picture." Alana said through giggles.

"This is not funny." I was never more serious in my life.

"Just take your BlackBerry. Please just do this for me. You're gonna be fine."

"What am I gonna tell the family? It's dark now and I'm lost. I'm alone."

"Angie, you're going to be fine."

I found out later, Alana had to tell all of 20th Century Fox that she wasn't able to attend the companywide staff meeting because her friend was having a panic attack in Amsterdam.

She stayed with me through the bus ride and my attempt to figure out if I had circled the same block three times. Every half block I questioned whether I was still going in the right direction.

Finally, I made it home, where Mama Sacha helped me to the couch to watch TV with Grandma, who asked a lot of questions and told crazy stories that I couldn't understand at all.

Weeks later I found out my pot brownie came with a tax: A $2,000 cell phone bill.

TRIPPING POINT

Just say no to Space Cakes—and yes to good friends.

QUICK HITS | AMSTERDAM

ERICA BRAY | TRAVELZOO

…Nobody told me that Amsterdam was so beautiful and had so much cultural vitality (beyond the red light district and coffee shops). Be sure to check out Anne Frank's house **and eat lots of powdered pancakes**….

• •

HOLLY WIERSMA | PRODUCER

…**Hotel Romero is very cute and you can get good deals**. It is right across from the square where there are about 100 restaurants and bars….

• •

JOSH D. MEYERS | "MAD TV"

…I am who I am because of Boom Chicago. It's the Second Cityesque comedy theater started by Northwestern Grads some 20 years ago. They've just moved to a great old theater on the Rozengracht. Alumni are working all over the place in Hollywood now. My brother Seth, Jordan Peele from Key and Peele, Ike Barinholtz from the Mindy Project, the list goes on and on. I'd see a show there and then hop on a boat tour. But don't get on one of those glassed-in monstrosities where no one is ever smiling. Find a small open air boat and do it right. If you're feeling adventurous, take a day trip out the the Efteling. It's the Dutch amusement park where everything is gnomes, dwarves, and faeries. **And I'm not saying you need to bring a box of legally purchased magic truffles (formerly magic mushrooms) but it's certainly an option**…

• •

GARRETT HEDLUND | "TRON", "ON THE ROAD"

…Have a spliff, walk along the canal, and **dream of owning one of those damn beaten house boats**…

• •

CHARLEY WALTERS

…You must rent a bike and make it your main transport the entire time you're there. I took a longer **bike ride past tulips and windmills all the way to "Zandvoort ann Zee,"** which is one of the cutest beach towns you've ever seen. It takes 3 hours but is beautiful...

• •

CADE HUDSON | PUBLICIST

….After my senior year of high school me and 7 of my best guy friends who I had grown up with took a trip to Amsterdam or **"The Promise Land" is what I call it**. I remember getting off the plane and couldn't wait to go to my first Hash Coffee shop. We went to a place called 7TH Heaven located right off a major street called Spuistraat and Voorburwal. We walked in and ordered just about everything they would let us order and went to town…

TAYLOR MOMSEN | ACTOR

…**Go to the Pippie Longstocking Museum** and the Anne Frank Museum. I love the Pippie museum cus it made me feel like going into a magical land. Keep in mind I was 8….

ALAN POLSKY | PRODUCER

…People go to Amsterdam to let loose kinda like Vegas. **So you can talk to anyone, people are pretty cool**. Also make sure to get their French fries with mayo and DON'T forget to eat the fresh herring that you can get on the street. Amazing!! Take the Heineken tour…

WILL KOPELMAN | ART CURATOR

…Sounds touristy, but the Van Gogh Museum and the Anne Frank house are a must. The Sensei Seed Growing Company (across from the police station) is one of the better "coffee shops" around. **One thing for sure: If you are traveling alone in Amsterdam, BE SAFE.** The town is full of sketchy people after sundown…

CHAPTER 30 BRINGING THE ADVENTURE HOME, AKA "EEK, WORK!"

DESTINATION Los Angeles

INSPIRATION Finding inspiration from within at the Sprouse brothers' birthday party. Yes, really.

● ● ● ● ● ● ● ● ● ● ● ● ● ● ● ● ● ●

It took 10 days of being back for me to realize I was going to leave my job and, appropriately, 30 to actually tell my boss I was going to do it—to leave and follow the road less traveled, not that anyone ever knows exactly what that is.

My first day back was a daze. At 8:30 a.m., I was at my desk in the office on Sunset Boulevard. My plane had landed in Los Angeles just 8 hours earlier. Emails were downloading—100, 700, 1,200, finally 2000 unopened messages. I watched them flow by. Where to begin?

I flipped on my iTunes and chose Dizzee Rascal beats from my Europe Mix. It wasn't loud enough to drown out the stressed voices from around the office chattering about final reports and spreadsheets, so I turned it up higher and imagined I was back running along the cliff in Cinque Terre. That felt good—but it wasn't getting my emails read.

I was again the lost child from my first hours in London, dazed and confused, except now I was hiding out in my office. I wasn't ready to share—yes, totally unlike me. I wasn't sad or happy to be back. I just was. I was what?

Deep breath. I started skimming emails, hoping that going through the motions would bring back the workaholic within. I read one dull, unimportant email after another—delete, delete, delete. Occasionally something fun would come through—like an invite to Scott Caan's photography show and 30th birthday. Pre-trip Angie would have quickly responded, "thanks yes see you there," calendared it and moved on. But instead I clicked the link to Scott's gallery and buried myself in his images, including a beautiful black and white of an Amsterdam street with "30" as a house number. (A print of the photograph now hangs in my house.) Forty-five minutes later, I still hadn't read any more emails and my mind was plotting my next adventure.

Finding Scott's photograph felt like a sign that a new, more integrated self had come back from the trip—the girl who chose her own adventure and made her own luck. But how could I reconcile her with the busy, successful PR connector with 2,000 emails?

The answer came five days after I was back. My company was throwing the Sprouse brothers' birthday party for Nintendo. Though I was barely back in the game and hadn't worked on the party, I was asked to come and help on site. Celebrity parents would be in attendance with their kids and there was going to be a lot of hoopla.

Day of, according to protocol, I arrived a little early to the event. As per usual pre-event, the girls from the office were flitting about, juggling all the last-minute stresses of event production logistics, preparing the press and photographers—in short, making sure everything was perfect for the 16-year-old Nickelodeon twins' birthday.

Me, I felt like I was in slow-mo, watching myself outside my body, while the rest of the room sped around me.

I walked past the step and repeat—the big backdrop with brands that you see in red carpet photographs—and said hello at the check-in table. Two assistants almost knocked me over, rushing past me to reinforce the backdrop with extra tape.

Entering the main party area, I saw one of the first DJs I'd ever met, Ryan Best. Happiness filled me as I ran over, excited to tell him about all the new sounds I'd heard spinning in Europe. I felt myself coming back to life and excitement returning. Just as I was telling him my story of meeting Dizzee, we heard my name being yelled—more of a summons than a request.

"ANGIE, we NEED your help. Can you go figure out the lighting? We have FIVE MINUTES before guests start arriving and it's TOO LIGHT!! Hurry PLEASE!"

"Of course."

I turned to Ryan and shrugged, mouthing, "I'll be back."

I spoke to someone about the lighting, but completely forgot about follow through when I ran into Megan, the Sprouse's publicist.

"Angie! It's been so long! How are you? I want you to meet my fiancé!"

Megan had always been a favorite publicist of mine. She didn't bullshit or fake it. She was good at her job.

"You're engaged!? I'd love to meet him!!" Megan brought me over to talk to her soon-to-be husband and it wasn't long before we were all sharing travel stories.

Then, suddenly, guests were arriving. Tons of kids and their parents were standing around in the main event area. The DJ was playing but no one was dancing. They were all standing around, looking a little awkward under the lights that were—uh-oh—still a little too bright. My colleagues shot me evil looks, frustrated and worried the event would be a bust.

I felt Angie Panicki bubbling up inside. But then my eyes fell on Ryan, who smiled at me. I remembered our earlier conversation and a light went on inside.

I rushed across the room and he took off his earphones.

"Play Dizzee!"

As the sounds of one of my favorite songs from Europe blared, I took to the dance floor and started pulling kids in with me. I pulled out my video camera and the kids, born performers, immediately kicked things up a notch. Within 10 minutes, every single Disney star in the joint was dancing in a circle around Willow Smith, and I was right there with them.

When I finally took a breather, Megan smiled and squeezed my shoulder.

"Angie, you did it! You saved the party! They're all dancing!"

And she was right. By being 100 percent myself—trip self, Angie self, authentic self, whatever it was—I made the evening fun for everyone, including myself. I had already realized while traveling that I would always love the people side of my job, and didn't want to leave it. Now I saw that Trip Angie wasn't in the way of me being successful at that— she made me even better.

I took some days to turn things over, but eventually realized what I needed was enough independence to build more travel and writing into my life than H&S would ever allow. I wanted total freedom, or as close as I could get, to keep on making my own luck. I also wanted to be the one bringing on the challenges to overcome, not my employer. I knew now I was up for it.

I took a few more days to get my life organized and my fear in check—then I finally quit. Signing clients on my own came easily, in large part thanks to my incredible network, all the same people who had helped me reinvent my life through my trip. Of course, most of the real change has come in the years since. Change takes time. It hasn't all been easy, but my 30 Before 30 set the conditions right to make it all happen. The journey reminded me that I could control my own destiny. I could still choose to be Workaholic Angie. And I could pick and choose my own adventures when Workaholic Angie got overwhelmed.

Since then I've been lucky to travel to places like Greece, Australia, and India when I feel my soul needing a dose of travel to realign myself. I also slowly realized that one trip doesn't change who you are, but it will remind you of the things you love best about yourself. I've learned to explore and draw out those things, and help friends do the same. I've found ways to connect with the people in my life besides inviting them to parties. I started reading tarot cards and realized I didn't always have to be the one at the party dancing. Sometimes I could be the one in the corner, listening and giving advice to one person.

And most importantly, I learned what to do with emotions, both the happy ones and the big, wet teary kind that I used to ignore or run through. Now I share them, and share them broadly. The more I tell, the quicker I heal. And, just as they did when I announced the 30 Before 30, my friends and loved ones have always answered my call with good humor, love, and booty shaking—when I need it.

TRIPPING POINT

Travel is more than a vacation. It's inspiration, it's adventure, and it's a book of memories that can lead to an entirely new story back at home.

ACKNOWLEDGEMENTS

Thank you to the people who listened, read, and encouraged me. I look back and truly see that this book is a beautiful mishmash of inspiration from so many people in my life. Mom and Dad. Adam and JJ and Aude. And every name in this book who allowed me to include them here!

To Sara Grace, who got it done. Andy Hyman for being the RomCom voiceover teacher in my head. Kristi Korzec. Laura Sandler, my screen-writer. Jean Kwolek. Jen Birn. Maggie Haynes. Page Farmer. Milana Rabkin. Liz Gemmill. Brooke Blumberg. Robbin Lang. Beth Shenberger. Colleen Kerwin. The Summit crew for constant support. Sarah Raimo, cheerleader. Alana Kleiman. Rachel Krupa. Camille Guaty. AJ Dipersia. Janae Twisselman. Alex Bard. John Palumbo. Katie Hartmen. Ali Puliti. Ellen Todras. Carlene Rowe. Daniel Ek. Kelly Shami. Joel Goldman. Rob Meder. Melissa Poh. Erica Cornwall. Amy Benziger. Frank E Flowers. Sarah Kruberg. Natalia Aranda. Whitney Jones. Chelsea Macdonald. Lani Tiberghien. Natalie Bond. Kristen McGuiness. Victor Saphire. Jamie Afifi. Arik Ruchim. Holly Wiersma. Robin Baum. Rachel Zalis. Virginia Trinkle. Cade Hudson. Molly Sims. Sam Hanks. Helena Pucavic. Jason Pomeranc. Jim Holleran. Steve Dennis. Anya Panteleyeva. Aron Levitz. Amy Martin. Isabel Calderon Bird. Terry Dougas. Noella Downs, for first telling me to write.

Finally, thanks to all the people who crossed my path on the trip and became part of the story.

CPSIA information can be obtained at www.ICGtesting.com
Printed in the USA
LVOW02s0027041213

363753LV00002B/4/P